C. C. BATES • MARYANN McBRIDE •

# THE NEXT STEP FORWARD IN
# RUNNING RECORDS

## GETTING TO THE HEART OF
## EFFECTIVE INSTRUCTION THROUGH
## DEEPER QUALITATIVE ANALYSIS

Publisher/Content editor: Lois Bridges
Editorial director: Sarah Longhi
Editor-in-chief/Development editor: Raymond Coutu
Production editor: Danny Miller
Senior editor: Shelley Griffin
Art director: Tom Martinez
Interior designer: Maria Lilja

*To all those who have influenced and continue to influence our thinking—our families, friends, colleagues, and students.*

# CONTENTS

**VIDEO LINKS**

Go to **scholastic.com/ResourcesNSFRR** to access this book's full menu of professional videos. Watch the authors take, score, and analyze running records, and make instructional decisions based on their findings.

# ACKNOWLEDGMENTS

First and foremost, we would like to acknowledge that we stand on the shoulders of many great leaders in the field of literacy. One person whose research and insights have framed our thinking and changed the course of our careers is Marie M. Clay. Our work has also been deeply influenced by former Reading Recovery® trainers at the Ohio State University, including Gay Su Pinnell, Carol Lyons, Diane DeFord, Rosemary Estes, and Mary Fried. They have taught us so much about the application of Clay's literacy processing theory and the close observation of children, paving the way for Reading Recovery in the United States.

We would like to acknowledge all those at Scholastic who helped us expand our ideas about the use of running records and their role in instructional decision making. We appreciate the team assembled to work on this book: Lois Bridges, Ray Coutu, Sarah Longhi, Shelley Griffin, and Maria Lilja. Thank you for your feedback, patience, and encouragement.

We would also like to thank the following educators for contributing photographs of their work with students for this book: Tammy Seals (cover and interior photos), Jesstina Bushery, Carolyn Gwinn, Lisa Hall, Sophie Kowzun, Leslie Lausten, Anselle Marisco, Heather Micheli, Pam O'Loughlin, Bonnie Porter, Julie Taylor, and Sandra Weaver. Special thanks to Hayley Hoover for her assistance.

Finally, we would like to thank our friends and family members who put up with us and supported us during the process of writing the manuscript and reviewing design stages. Denise, thank you for challenging us to refine our thinking. Cecil, thank you for your close read of the text and editorial suggestions. Daron, thank you for helping us remember to balance our personal and professional lives.

# INTRODUCTION

In the acclaimed children's book, *Seven Blind Mice*, Ed Young shares the story of a group of blind mice that set out to observe an unidentified "something." One by one, the mice return with a limited description of it. Over a week, the information builds and eventually the mice have a complete picture of the something. The mice's process can be likened to running records. If you examine a child's reading behaviors in a discrete and isolated way, it will provide an incomplete understanding of his or her processing. Each attempt the child makes while reading is important and leads to a comprehensive view of the child's reading ability. Take, for example, the following excerpt from a running record.

### *No More Training Wheels* by Anna Kim
### (Level E, running words: 107)
This is a story about a little girl who isn't sure she wants to give up her bike's training wheels, but her mother takes them off anyway, because she's confident her daughter doesn't need them. Below is a child's reading of the final page of the text, where the little girl realizes she can ride without training wheels.

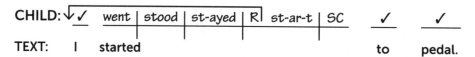

With his first attempt, *went*, the child anticipates the meaning of the story and uses a common language structure, but he realizes the word *went* is not visually correct. The second attempt, *stood*, shows visual similarity to *started* at the beginning and end, and maintains some meaning, moving the child closer to a correct solution. On the third attempt, *st-ayed*, the child isolates the consonant blend at the beginning and tries the long /a/ sound. To further integrate meaning and language structure, he rereads and then conducts a closer visual analysis across the word, left to right. The child's multiple attempts demonstrate the complexities of learning to read. Through qualitative analyses of the child's reading behaviors and attempts, a complete picture emerges, allowing teachers to make effective instructional decisions grounded in evidence.

# LEARNING FROM TEACHERS

Together, the three of us have over 100 years of experience teaching children and working with teachers nationwide. Taking, scoring, analyzing, and using running records is part of our everyday practice. We understand the challenges they present, but also know their instructional power. This book aims to help you understand and use running records as a tool to support readers in your classroom.

Running records, for the purposes of this book, refer to records on a child's second reading of a text. By analyzing the second attempt, we can focus on how the child is applying what we've taught him or her. For example, if during the first reading we taught how rereading allows the child to integrate the meaning of the story with the available visual and phonological information, we expect to observe this in the running record. If our teaching has been successful, the child should use the visual information to solve the word when he or she rereads the text.

We have organized this book into four color-coded parts to help you maximize your use of running records.

**PART I: Making the Case for Running Records** shares the research about the complexities of learning to read and why assessing oral reading behaviors gives us insight into this process.

**PART II: Taking, Scoring, and Analyzing Running Records** explains how to systematically record children's oral reading, calculate error and self-correction rates, and assess for fluency and comprehension.

**PART III: Making Informed Instructional Decisions Using Running Records** provides examples of how to plan next steps in your instruction, using the information from your running records.

**PART IV: Understanding Challenges Identified by Running Record Analysis** discusses specific issues related to reading and how to use running records with older striving readers.

In sections called "From Practice to Proficiency," you will have the opportunity to practice the concepts discussed in each part.

Our intent is to help you see how the details of taking running records fit within the overall picture of learning to read. Our goal is to support you and your students. Teaching children to read is our most important work and our greatest joy!

Welcome to our book!
C.C., Maryann, and Jan

# Making the Case for Running Records

The chapters in Part I provide a rationale for the use of running records. We begin by answering often-asked questions about when, with whom, and how often to administer them. We place running records within an instructional cycle to explain the connection between teacher observation and decision making. We also share the theoretical underpinnings of running records by discussing an integrated theory of reading. Part of that discussion includes misconceptions of MSV (meaning, structure, and visual information), including the role each of those sources of information plays in the qualitative analysis of children's oral reading.

**VIDEO LINK**

Visit **scholastic.com/ResourcesNSFRR** for professional videos of the authors taking, scoring, and analyzing running records.

# CHAPTER 1

# The Purpose of Running Records

When we know why we are implementing certain practices, it strengthens teaching and learning. Without a theory to underpin our work, we are simply going through the motions. Reflective practitioners are able to adapt instruction based on the needs of children because they have developed a rationale grounded in theory that connects content and pedagogical knowledge to their observations of individual children.

## LEARNING FROM CHILDREN:
## THE POWER OF SYSTEMATIC OBSERVATION

The mice in Ed Young's *Seven Blind Mice* learned that the big picture is important, but so are the details. As teachers, we must be aware of both. We must understand the reading continuum and how children's individual behaviors contribute to their ongoing progress. Learning to read is complex. Without observation, we can be left in the dark, guessing at the "something," like Ed Young's mice. Learning from children begins with systematic observation (Clay, 2001). Running records enable us to capture, code, and analyze our observations of children's reading behaviors in the moment. With them, our observations become both a permanent record and a tool for understanding how children process text. We observe where and when the reading work is easy for children and where and when it isn't. We observe what they have under control and what they find confusing. Our observations, captured in running records, provide a unique view into how a child processes continuous text and help us determine our next steps.

## Observational Tools

There are many observational tools designed to help us understand a child's reading process. While they differ slightly in format and specific purpose, they are all intended to inform our instructional decision making. In the table below, we highlight the most widely used oral reading assessments. Each one is administered individually and requires the child to read aloud as the teacher observes his or her decoding skills, use of language and structure, fluency, and the construction of meaning as a feed-forward mechanism to anticipate, and a form of feedback for monitoring and self-correcting. The results of the assessments are often used for grouping and instructional planning purposes.

| Tool | Definition | Use | Considerations |
|---|---|---|---|
| **Running Record** (familiar read) | A written record of an oral reading. The passage used has been previously *read one time* by the student. After the reading, the teacher engages the student in conversation about the text to check understandings. An accuracy and self-correction rate are computed, and the errors and self-corrections are coded and analyzed. A note about the child's reading fluency is also recorded. | To gain information about the child's strategic reading behavior. Running records are used for instructional purposes and for progress monitoring. | Running records on familiar text are used frequently and are part of an ongoing cycle of instruction. Running records on familiar text do not need to be taken on every child every day but should be used as a tool by the teacher when problem-solving how to support children. This type of running record should not be used as a benchmark assessment to ascertain a child's reading level. While the accuracy rate for the reading is calculated, it isn't used for testing purposes. |

| Tool | Definition | Use | Considerations |
|---|---|---|---|
| **Running Record** (cold read) | A written record of an oral reading of a passage that *has not been previously read* by the student. After the reading, the teacher engages the student in conversation about the text to check understandings. Accuracy and self-correction rates are computed, and the errors and self-corrections are coded and analyzed. A note about the child's reading fluency is also recorded. | To assess the child's reading level and strategic behaviors on novel text | Running records on unseen text can be used for testing purposes. |
| **Benchmark Assessment** | A collection of leveled texts set aside for the purpose of testing. Benchmark assessments may include letter, sound, and word identification, decoding skills, fluency and reading rate, and comprehension. Typically, the assessment also includes a running record of an unseen text. The benchmark assessment usually features accompanying forms, which contain the preprinted text. Teachers use the forms to mark the student's reading behaviors, including errors and self-corrections. | To assess the child's skills and determine his or her independent and instructional text reading levels | A benchmark assessment is often administered at the beginning, middle, and end of the year, and results are sometimes communicated to parents on student report cards. Benchmark assessments can be time-consuming. |

| Tool | Definition | Use | Considerations |
|------|-----------|-----|----------------|
| **Miscue Analysis** | A procedure designed to identify how readers process written language by analyzing errors or *miscues*—"departures from the written text." Miscues, according to Goodman and Goodman (1977), are not usually random, because they reflect what children know about the meaning, syntax, and graphophonic nature of written language. Following the oral reading, the student provides an unassisted retelling. The miscues are then coded by a set of questions that determine the parts of the process for which the reader has control. Additionally, the teacher notes whether the miscue either preserves or interferes with the meaning of the passage. | To gain insight into the child's psycholinguistic processing and the interaction between thought and language | Miscue analysis has greatly contributed to the role language plays in reading but does not place emphasis on children's decoding skills. A formal miscue analysis can be time-consuming, but several effective adaptations exist—such as "Over-the-Shoulder Miscue Analysis" (Davenport, 2002; Harvey & Ward, 2017) and "Skinny Miscue Analysis" (Stephens, 2019)—that don't take as much time. |
| **Informal Reading Inventories** (e.g., Qualitative Reading Inventory) | A grade-level reading assessment that measures word recognition, vocabulary, comprehension, and oral reading accuracy. Informal reading inventories range from pre-primer to high school. Students may be asked to read orally or silently. After the passage is read, the teacher asks explicit and implicit questions. | To determine if children are reading on grade level | Most informal inventories offer three to six passages at each level, which may not accurately identify the specific level at which children are reading. |

PART I

# RUNNING RECORDS AS PART
# OF THE INSTRUCTIONAL CYCLE

In this book, we explore how analyzing running records using a familiar text can support students' strategic reading behaviors and how your findings can inform individual and small-group instruction. Running records begin the instructional cycle, so it is important to figure out how they fit in your daily routine.

## When Should I Take Running Records?

Running records can be taken during an individual conference or small-group instruction. When you take them during small-group instruction, have other students work independently while you quickly take a record on one child. This can occur before, during, or at the end of the lesson. To avoid interruptions such as, "I am finished. Now what?", think carefully about what you give the other children to read while you take the record. You may have children read a text at their independent level so they will not require your assistance. You could also engage them in some type of writing extension inspired by a text they've read, such as composing and illustrating their understandings of it. Keep in mind that efficient use of time is a major factor when taking running records in a classroom setting. If the children in the group get restless, they will require your attention, and you may need to put the record aside and return to it later.

Another option for taking a running record during small-group instruction is to limit the length of each record. For example, after taking a record on Child 1 for 2–3 pages, you would take a record on Child 2 reading 2–3 pages. Because the children are reading simultaneously but not chorally, they will finish at different rates. So, it's okay to have the group reread the book if you are still taking a record on a child. However, don't ask the children to read the book more than twice because they will tire of the text, which can lead to behavior management issues. Be sure to wrap things up quickly.

For children learning to read or reading books that contain fewer than 100 words, take the record on their reading of the complete text. As they begin reading longer, more complex texts, you may want to carefully select a 100-word excerpt that captures the gist and meaning of the story as accurately as possible. For nonfiction, select a 100-word excerpt that communicates information about a concept or idea.

With practice, you will increase your proficiency in taking running records and decrease the amount of time it requires.

## With Whom and How Often Should I Take Running Records?

Teachers are often told to take running records on every child in their classroom, but it is more beneficial to think about where children are on the continuum and why a record may be useful. You will likely need to take running records on young children and striving readers more frequently than on older, proficient readers. The chart below offers some guidelines for taking running records based on text level and grade level, but decisions should always be made on a case-by-case basis. Keep in mind that leveled text is only one type of text that should be used in a comprehensive approach to classroom instruction.

| Text Level | Grade Level | Frequency of Running Record | Rationale |
|---|---|---|---|
| **A–C** | Kindergarten | Weekly | Observe children's directional movement of print and voice-to-print match. Running records on Level C texts will also begin to provide additional information on strategic processing, problem solving, knowledge of high-frequency words, and use of letter-sound information. Observe children to ensure they are looking at the print and not just using the pictures to construct meaning. |
| **D–J** | Grade 1 | Weekly at first, and then at least monthly. Continue with weekly monitoring if children are making slow progress. | Watch out for memorization at the beginning of this range, especially in texts with repetitive patterns. Rapid changes occur during these levels. Observe and take note of risk-taking, problem-solving actions, fluency, and comprehension for evidence of change over time. |
| **K–P** | Grades 2 and 3 | Beginning, middle, and end of year. For children still experiencing some difficulty, use weekly running records to guide instruction. | Running records at these levels can provide a check on children's integrated processing, and give insight into their flexible use of visual information on multisyllabic words. |
| **Q+** | Grade 4 and Higher | Take a modified running record as needed on a portion of the text. | Most children at these levels are conventional readers, reading quickly and accurately. Note how they monitor and solve unfamiliar, multisyllabic words. |

Our correlations of text levels and grade levels may not apply for striving readers. Children having difficulty, regardless of age or grade level, need tailored instruction that results from *closely observing* their reading behaviors and how those behaviors change over time. Running records provide a window into a child's processing and will help you determine instructional next steps.

## Where Do Running Records Fit Into the Instructional Cycle?

Once you have decided when and with whom to take a running record, think about where running records fit into the instructional cycle. As we stated earlier, running records can be used to begin an instructional cycle, to monitor teaching and learning, and to subsequently begin again by generating a new cycle. The information gleaned from your records should inform individual, small-group, and whole-class instruction. Furthermore, what you learn from running records can also provide support for children's independent practice.

The cycle for taking a running record is illustrated in the chart below. Immediately after taking a running record, you can provide targeted, in-the-moment instruction that meets each student's individual needs. You then analyze the record and compare it to other records from the same child, from other children in the same group, and from other children in the class. This kind of reflective practice allows you to develop an instructional plan. The plan should include decisions about book choice, letter and word work, vocabulary and language structures to address, and opportunities to teach for strategic action.

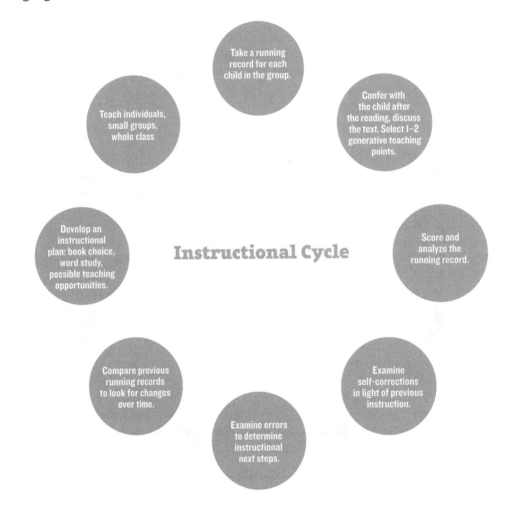

Take a running record for each child in the group.

Confer with the child after the reading, discuss the text. Select 1–2 generative teaching points.

Teach individuals, small groups, whole class

Score and analyze the running record.

Develop an instructional plan: book choice, word study, possible teaching opportunities.

**Instructional Cycle**

Examine self-corrections in light of previous instruction.

Compare previous running records to look for changes over time.

Examine errors to determine instructional next steps.

When applying this instructional cycle to a group of students, consider what you've learned from the running records of all the children in the group. For example, if you notice that children are making errors on high-frequency words, you will want to dedicate instructional time to teaching appropriate high-frequency words.

## CLOSING THOUGHT

Children must be able to see themselves in the texts they read and connect to characters and experiences on a personal and intimate level. Rudine Sims Bishop's (1990) work—her metaphor of windows, mirrors, and sliding glass doors—was groundbreaking and central to the conversation about diversity in literature for young readers. When we analyze a running record, we are reminded that Marie Clay called upon a similar metaphor, describing the errors and self-corrections children make as misty *windows* into their processing. We also know that running records are *mirrors* serving as reflections of our teaching. Finally, the running record is like a *sliding glass door*. A sliding glass door permits a view like a window, is reflective like a mirror, but also offers a passageway. Intentional, targeted instruction guides students through the door as they journey to lead literate lives.

# CHAPTER 2

# The Misunderstanding of MSV: Making the Case for Running Records

Recently, social media posts and blogs have been critical of the "three-cueing theory," or MSV, claiming it is an ineffective way to teach reading (Hanford, 2019; Schwartz & Sparks, 2019). Those critiques, sometimes written by journalists and appearing in non-peer-reviewed sources, have gained momentum and are influencing education policy and practice. To make the case for why running records should be part of our assessment and instructional practices, it is important to understand MSV.

The three-cueing theory, a phrase often used interchangeably with MSV, is not a theoretical model of reading, nor is it a method of or approach to the teaching of reading. It is a way of recording and analyzing students' errors and self-corrections. It enables us to examine the sources of information young readers use or neglect while they are reading:

**M:** meaning or semantics
**S:** structure or syntax
**V:** visual and phonological aspects of print

Using codes, we record the systematic observation of oral reading behaviors and analyze how students are monitoring their reading and processing written language (reading is a language process—together with writing, speaking and listening), to support instructional decision making.

## AN INTEGRATED THEORY OF READING

MSV is grounded in an integrated theoretical model of reading, which is derived from observational and experimental research (Clay, 1966, 2001; Compton-Lilly, 2020; Doyle, 2019; Rumelhart, 1994; Schwartz & Gallant, 2011; Sirinides, Gray & May, 2018; Wixson & Lipson, 1991; What Works Clearinghouse, 2013). An integrated theory of reading values students' meaning-making process and promotes reading for understanding, which occurs by flexibly integrating multiple information sources. Reading is more than decoding. Of course, readers make "decisions regarding perceptions of letter features, letter sounds, letter clusters," but they also evaluate and confirm or revise words "in conjunction with decisions regarding syntactic information, at either a phrase or clause level, and decisions on the basis of semantic information, which is more general knowledge of the topic or genre" (Doyle, 2019, p. 92). An integrated theory of reading recognizes children's use of multiple information sources and underpins the practical implications of using MSV as a way to understand and support beginning readers.

### More Than Accuracy

So how has the use of MSV become so misunderstood? One answer may have to do with how running records are used. Some teachers are only recording children's oral reading errors and self-corrections to calculate an accuracy rate and determine a reading level. Assigning a text level to a child because he or she reads a book at a particular accuracy rate does not result in instructional implications. In fact, basing a reading level solely on accuracy rate is very misleading. Take, for example, a child with a great interest in football. The child may find a text about a football game engaging. He or she may be familiar with vocabulary in the book such as *gridiron*, *interception*, and *fumble*. Because those words are part of the child's everyday language, the text is automatically more accessible. For another child, with no interest in or experience with football, the text is likely to be more difficult, even though it would be considered an appropriate level based on his or her running record accuracy rate. Reading is a complex process, and we shouldn't limit a child's reading to a level. Furthermore, only using an accuracy rate derived from a running record could be an indication that a teacher may not fully understand the complexities involved with the processing of written language and, therefore, may not see the value in using MSV for analysis.

Most running record templates include a column for capturing a child's errors and self-corrections by circling M, S, or V. But capturing information and engaging in the in-depth analysis and reflection about how that information can support instructional decision making are two very different tasks. If we view the analysis of sources of information young readers are using and neglecting as perfunctory, it is no wonder that the use of running records for assessment and instruction is in question. Limiting a running record to an accuracy rate strips it of its real power and promotes a reductionist view that contributes to the misunderstandings of those who are critical of it.

## Literacy Processing

When we code and analyze students' reading behaviors, we gain a better understanding of their literacy processing. Literacy processing, as defined by Clay (2001), involves the "in the head" working systems we use to problem-solve when reading. The constructive reader assembles and reassembles neural networks to solve increasingly complex text by integrating perceptual, cognitive, and linguistic behaviors (Clay, 2001).

Literacy processing differs from a model of reading that promotes decoding as a precursor to comprehension. For example, the "science of reading" perspective focuses solely on the decoding of words and fails to recognize the importance of monitoring in word recognition (Schwartz, 1997). Word recognition, however, requires both the searching and use of information sources in initial attempts, and the monitoring of those attempts for accuracy (McGee, Kim, Nelson & Fried, 2015; Schwartz & Gallant, 2011). When beginning readers make initial attempts at unknown words, they often use limited visual information in combination with meaning and structure because they are still learning about letters and sounds. The attempts are not "lost learning trials" as some might suggest (Petscher et al., 2020, p. 16). Instead, as children monitor sound-to-letter expectations, they begin to self-correct. The acts of searching, monitoring, and self-correcting contribute to children's developing orthographic knowledge, strengthening it over time. As orthographic knowledge grows, children rely on it more in their initial reading attempts and are more likely to use meaning and language structure to guide comprehension.

# UNPACKING MSV—OR "VMS"

We wrote this book to help teachers better understand the complexity of reading and the power of closely observing children's oral reading behaviors, especially as they relate to the use of visual information (V). Critics of MSV argue that it doesn't emphasize phonics enough, with some even citing the position of the V at the end of "MSV" as proof of its inferiority when, in fact, MSV is listed alphabetically. We will refer to MSV and not VMS, but because of the heightened concern about the teaching of phonics, we will begin by unpacking the visual information.

## Visual

V, or the visual information, stands for the ways in which children draw upon the alphabetic principle, or the connection between letters and sounds. V also includes children's use of orthographic patterns and their automatic recognition of high-frequency words. It does not involve illustrations, as much as its name may suggest it does. If a child attempts a word, takes his eyes off the text, searches an illustration, and goes back and attempts to read the word, it is not coded as the use of visual information.

Let's examine a child's reading of page 5 of *All About Spiders* by Violet Findley (Level E; running words: 114). Notice her use of visual information is clearly recorded, including her attention to high-frequency words and her decoding efforts. Examine how the child read the text and what we recorded, using the following questions to guide you.

- How is the child using the visual information when reading?
- What are the instructional implications?

| Text | Student Says | Running Record |
|---|---|---|
| See this spider? | See the spider | ✓ the ✓ / this |
| It is hiding on a flower. | It is hiding in/on a flower. | ✓ ✓ ✓ in \|SC ✓ ✓ / on\| |
| Some spiders are good at hiding. | Some spiders are good at hiding. | ✓ ✓ ✓ ✓ ✓ ✓ |
| Hiding helps them stay safe. | Hiding helps them st-ay/ stay s-a-f. Hiding helps them stay safe. | ✓ ✓ ✓ st-ay✓ s-a-f \|R\|SC / stay safe \| \| |

On the first line of the text, the child reads *the* for *this* and does not self-correct the error. Because the substitution does not interfere with meaning and fits grammatically, the child lets it go. High-frequency words that begin with *th* are often difficult for children, especially at this early level. Maybe you have had a student who goes through every *th* word possible before settling on one. Recording those types of substitutions provides insight for instruction and signals a need for more practice with visually similar words.

On the second line, the child self-corrects when reading *in* for *on*. Again, those are visually similar words and also words that the child has been encountering in early-level texts. While we are satisfied with the self-correction, eventually the word should be recognized quickly and accurately on the first attempt. Practice with high-frequency words will help the child recognize them automatically and support her use of visual information.

On the final line, the child also demonstrates her understanding of decoding and knowledge of phonics. When reading the word *stay*, she takes it apart using efficient units *st-ay*. When she comes to *safe*, she uses the short-*a* sound in her initial attempt and then monitors and rereads, self-correcting the word and showing her flexibility as a reader who knows the different sounds /a/ can produce. This self-correction has high tutorial value for the child. Children often practice reading short- and long-vowel words in isolation, but switching between short and long vowels when reading continuous text emphasizes the need for flexibility when decoding. While the child clearly uses visual information in the attempt using the short vowel, her use of meaning and rereading supports her decoding flexibility.

## Meaning

As children engage with text, they use meaning to guide their reading and construct understandings. Meaning can occur at the paragraph, sentence, phrase, and word level, and has to fit with the overarching view of the text, which is often referred to as the gist. For example, if a child reads *The house is brown* for *The horse is brown*, we could say, "Yes, that sentence makes sense. A house could be brown." However, if the story is about horses, the larger context or gist of the text must be considered. While the error may make sense at the sentence level, it does not make sense at the text level.

Meaning is influenced by the setting, the traits and roles of characters, and the structures related to the story (e.g., problem and solution; or time sequences, such as days of the week, seasons, or periods during the day—morning, afternoon, evening.) Readers' conceptual understandings, background knowledge about informational topics, vocabulary, and lived experiences assist them in extracting and making meaning while reading. Therefore, when children are learning to read, we should encourage them to make sense of text while simultaneously using the visual information.

Let's examine a child's reading of page 6 of *Going to Grandma's House* by Tim Barber (Level C; running words: 83). Notice the child's substitution and how it was recorded, using the following questions to guide you.

- How is the child using meaning when reading?
- What are the instructional implications?

| Text | Student Says | Running Record |
| --- | --- | --- |
| **My sister gave me my pajamas.** | My sister gave me my clothes. | ✓ ✓ ✓ ✓ ✓ $\frac{clothes}{pajamas}$ |
| **I put them in my backpack.** | I put them in my backpack. | ✓ ✓ ✓ ✓ ✓ ✓ |

The child shows he is engaged with the story while reading. His substitution of *clothes* for *pajamas* reflects an understanding that the character will need additional clothing when going to visit Grandma. Spending the night with a grandparent or other loved one is a common early-childhood experience and requires planning and packing. It makes sense that the child in the story will need extra clothes. When reading early-level texts, children often search the picture when they come to an unknown word. This searching behavior is linked to meaning-making, and while it has a place in learning to read, it shouldn't replace ongoing thinking about the story as a way of holding onto meaning as the narrative unfolds. In this example, the child looked at the picture before saying *clothes*. The running record doesn't indicate that the child checked the attempt against the letters and sounds in the word *pajamas*. For beginning readers, cross-checking meaning against visual information is an important early behavior and, in this example, would be an excellent teaching point.

## Structure

Structure has to do with language and the grammar that governs it. Sometimes the structures that appear in text do not match children's oral language structures. In other words, the language used by children in conversation may vary from the language used in the books they are reading. While it is important to honor language variations, when children are learning to read, they have to learn to coordinate what they say with the visual information presented in the text. As texts become progressively more challenging, so do the grammatical and literary structures. A child's ear for increasingly complex structures is developed through conversations in which new and unusual structures are used. It is also developed through read-alouds of high-quality literature, which expose children to literary language, paving the way for them to control more advanced structures in their own reading. Additionally, structure and meaning are closely tied; a child's use of structure often gives insight into the ways in which he or she is making meaning.

Let's examine a child's reading from a simple teacher-made text. This text was written by the child's teacher because the child was particularly interested in fishing with his father. Teacher-made texts are discussed in Chapter 11. Examine the reading using the following questions as a guide.

- What do you notice about the child's errors?
- How is the child using structure when reading?
- What are the instructional implications?

| Text | Student Says | Running Record |
|---|---|---|
| **I like fishing.** | I like fishing. | ✓ ✓ ✓ |
| **Where is my fishing rod?** | Where is my fishing rod? | ✓ ✓ ✓ ✓ ✓ |
| **Where is the hook?** | Where is the hook? | ✓ ✓ ✓ ✓ |
| **Where is the worm?** | Where is the worm? | ✓ ✓ ✓ ✓ |
| **Where are the fish?** | Where is the fish? | ✓ is/are ✓ ✓ |
| **Oh, no!** | | |
| **Where are the fish?** | Oh no | ✓ ✓ |
| **Here come the fish.** | Where is the fish? | ✓ is/are ✓ ✓ |
| | Here comes the fish. | ✓ comes/come ✓ ✓ |

The child may not yet understand that the word *fish* is both singular and plural. Children develop understandings of the grammatical constraints of language as part of their oral language development. Those understandings are then carried forward into their reading. A child who still sees the word *fish* as one fish and not many would then likely use the verb *is* instead of *are*. This hypothesis is confirmed when the child reads *comes* for *come*, as *comes* agrees with *fish* as a singular noun. The child has used his knowledge of structure and his implicit understanding that when a noun is singular, the verb must also be singular. Solidifying his high-frequency word base would help him as his developing understandings of structure expand. In this case, if the child knew the high-frequency word *are*, he could likely override his oral language structure and recognize that some nouns have an irregular plural form.

## CLOSING THOUGHT

While we have unpacked the sources of information individually in this chapter, it is important to keep in mind that the interaction and integration of MSV is the ultimate goal in literacy processing. Using running records to capture the sources of information used and neglected by children helps us to choose the types of text to use for reading instruction, think about ways to introduce texts, and determine the types of scaffolding we provide.

In Part II, we focus on the fundamentals for taking and scoring a running record. We also move beyond those fundamentals to show you how to better understand children's literacy processing systems, and how your instructional decisions can contribute to supporting children's reading progress.

# Taking, Scoring, and Analyzing Running Records

Throughout Part II, we share our insights, based on years of experience working with teachers and children, to highlight how taking, scoring, and analyzing running records reveal the next steps for instruction.

We start by showing you a standard way of recording a child's oral reading. The examples used come from real children interacting with real fiction and nonfiction texts. Studying them, along with our guidelines, will deepen your understanding of how a child's literacy processing system supports his or her problem solving while reading. The examples also show how the consistent coding and scoring of running records enables you to link assessment to instruction. Finally, we discuss the role of fluency and comprehension in reading and suggest ways to capture them in your running records.

 **VIDEO LINK**
Visit **scholastic.com/ResourcesNSFRR** for professional videos of the authors taking, scoring, and analyzing running records.

# CHAPTER 3
# Taking a Running Record

Becoming proficient at taking running records requires an understanding of children's reading behaviors and a consistent way to code those behaviors. The process is not as easy as it may seem, and it takes time. In his book *Outliers: The Story of Success*, Malcolm Gladwell states that there are no instant experts. To be successful, you have to put in the time. Practice is something we often recommend to children and parents. Have you ever told your students that the more you read, the better a reader you become? Well, the same is true for running records. The more you practice taking, scoring, and analyzing them, the better you become at using them to inform instruction.

One part of becoming proficient is learning to juggle taking running records in a classroom with a lot happening around you. It's critical to establish routines and procedures in your daily schedule for running records. Explain to the children that what you are doing is important and that they should not interrupt. Creating a classroom community where the work of each reader is respected sends a strong message to all children about the importance of the reading process.

# WHY WE USE A STANDARD SET OF CODES

When we take a running record, we use a standard set of codes that represents how a child reads each word in a text. When we review a running record, the codes enable us to recreate the reading verbatim, while at the same time providing a common language when reflecting on practice with our colleagues and discussing next steps for children.

In addition to recording how the child reads each word, we note other behaviors, such as comments the child makes. The child may overtly state that something is not right. He or she may comment on the complex problem solving he or she is doing. Children's comments provide insight into the ways they are working on the details of print.

The following general understandings pave the way for the accurate and consistent recording of children's reading behaviors. The recommendations in this chapter are based on the work of Marie Clay (2019) and her *Observation Survey of Early Literacy Achievement*. The coding has been used for decades and captures the complexities of the reading process.

## Running Record Template

When you're ready to take running records with your students, use the template that appears in Appendix B on pages 235–237 and at scholastic.com/ResourcesNSFRR.

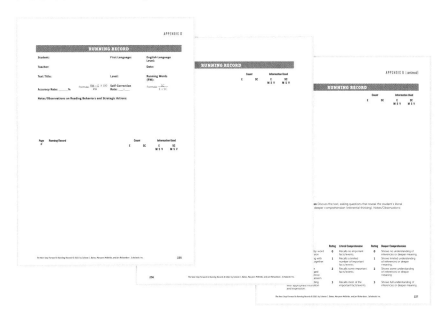

# Running Record Codes

| Student Behaviors | Definition | How to Record |
|---|---|---|
| **Frequent Actions** | | |
| **Correct Response** | Child reads exactly what is in the text | ✓ |
| **Substitution** | Child replaces a word in the text with another word or an attempt | $\dfrac{\text{child's response}}{\text{text}}$ |
| **Self-Correction** | Child fixes an error with the correct word | SC |
| **Adding and Skipping Words** | | |
| **Insertion** | Child adds a word not in the text | $\dfrac{\text{word inserted}}{\text{-}}$ |
| **Omission** | Child skips a word | $\dfrac{\text{-}}{\text{word omitted}}$ |
| **Repetitions and Rereadings** | | |
| **Repetition of a Correct Response** | Child repeats the word | R |
| **Repetition of a Substitution** | Child repeats the substitution | R |
| **Multiple Repetitions of a Correct Response** | Child repeats the word more than once (number indicates how many times the word is repeated) | $R_2, R_3$ |
| **Multiple Repetitions of a Substitution** | Child repeats the substitution more than once (number indicates how many times the word is repeated) | $R_2, R_3$ |
| **Repetition of More Than One Word** | Child repeats two or more words together (mark the words that were repeated) | ↓⌐⌐ R |
| **Repetition of More Than One Word With a Self-Correction on the Rereading** | Child self-corrects while rereading (mark the words that were repeated, drop a line facing down where the child self-corrects and label SC) | ↓⌐⌐ R SC |
| **Word Analysis and Multiple Attempts** | | |
| **Decoding Attempt** | Child tries sounds to get to the word | $\dfrac{\text{n- n-}}{\text{correct word}}$ |
| **Multiple Decoding Attempts** | Child makes multiple attempts on the same word | $\dfrac{\text{st - ay | stay - ing}}{\text{staying}}$ |
| **Spelling Out a Word** | Child says each letter name | $\dfrac{\text{G-O}}{\text{go}}$ |
| **Requests for Help or No Action** | | |
| **Appeal** | Child asks for help | $\dfrac{\text{A}}{\text{correct word}}$ |
| **Told** (correct word is said by the teacher) | Child is unable to continue, and the teacher tells the word | $\dfrac{\phantom{x}}{\text{T}}$ |
| **You Try It** (said by the teacher) | Teacher says "You try it" if the child makes no attempt and appeals for help | $\dfrac{\phantom{x}}{\text{Y}}$ |

# GENERAL UNDERSTANDINGS

It is helpful to remember a few things when taking running records. Most important, do not interrupt the student to do any teaching, as this is a time to observe what he or she does while reading. To begin, record above the line what the student says during the oral reading, and record below the line what the text says (or your response to the student's behavior).

*Student Response*
_____
*Text or Teacher Response*

When a child makes multiple attempts at a word, use a vertical line to separate each attempt, with the word from the text and your responses below the horizontal line. This is done to recreate the reading as it occurred in real time. Doing this captures the child's engagement with the text in an episodic way and allows you to better understand exactly what he or she did while reading the text.

## Running Record Rules: Capturing What the Child Says and the Text Says

The child says the word *jacket,* but the text says *coat.* Write the word *jacket,* draw a line under it, and write the word *coat* under the line.

*jacket*
_____
*coat*

The child then says *sweater.* Record the child's attempts, separating each one with a vertical line. Below the line, add the word from the text.

*jacket* | *sweater*
_____
*coat*  |

When taking a running record, each mark should mirror the number of words in the line and the number of lines on the page. To clarify, the marks should not be continuous but instead reflect the way the words appear in the book.

Be sure to leave plenty of space between the marks for greater visual clarity. For example, on page 3 of *Rainbow Day* by Megan Duhamel (Level D; running words: 81), the first line has four words, and the second and third lines each have five. On the next page are two examples of running records of a child's accurate reading. The first example captures the correct number of words on the page, but not the correct layout. The second example captures both the correct number of words and the correct number of lines.

Following the line and page layout makes scoring and analyzing the record easier because you can pinpoint the child's responses.

**EXAMPLE 1:** Incorrect
p. 3

✓ ✓ ✓ ✓ ✓ ✓ ✓ ✓ ✓ ✓

**EXAMPLE 2:** Correct
p. 3

✓ ✓ ✓ ✓

✓ ✓ ✓ ✓ ✓

✓ ✓ ✓ ✓ ✓

When taking a running record, it is sometimes difficult to keep up with the child. Leaving plenty of space between the marks and following the line and page layout allows you to go back and add details that you may not have captured. Further, following the line and page layout simplifies finding possible examples for your teaching points.

In the example on the next page, the teacher only had time to write what the child said, *my*, and draw a line under it. Because she followed the line and page layout and left extra space, it was easier to go back and add the word from the text.

**EXAMPLE 1:** Incorrect
p. 3

✓ ✓ ✓ ✓ ✓ ✓  my  ✓ ✓ ✓ ✓ ✓
                the

**EXAMPLE 2:** Correct
p. 3

✓ ✓ ✓ ✓

✓ ✓ ✓  my  ✓
        the

✓ ✓ ✓ ✓ ✓

In the previous examples, the running records represent a child's reading of a single page in *Rainbow Day*. When taking a record on a child's reading of multiple pages of a book, which is typically the case, separate the records for each page with a horizontal line. The lines serve as visual reminders of the book's page breaks.

p. 4

✓ ✓ ✓ ✓

✓ ✓ ✓ ✓ ✓

✓ ✓ ✓ ✓ ✓

p. 5

✓ ✓ ✓ ✓

✓ ✓ ✓ ✓ ✓

✓ ✓ ✓ ✓ ✓

# RECORDING STUDENT BEHAVIORS

In this section, we cover the standard coding of student behaviors, including frequent actions (e.g., correct response, substitution, self-correction), adding and skipping words, repetitions, decoding attempts, appeals, and teacher responses to student appeals. Examples are based on a child's reading of *Rainbow Day*.

## Frequent Actions

### Correct Response

When a child reads a word, use a check mark (✓) to indicate that the word was read correctly.

| Text | Student Says | How to Record |
|---|---|---|
| **It is a rainy day.** | It is a rainy day. | ✓ ✓ ✓ ✓ ✓ |

### Substitution

When a child reads one word for another, it is considered a substitution. To record the incorrect response, write the child's substitution, draw a line under it, and write the correct word below the line.

| Text | Student Says | How to Record |
|---|---|---|
| **I need my coat.** | I need my jacket. | ✓ ✓ ✓ jacket / coat |

### Self-Correction

When a child reads a word incorrectly and then immediately corrects the error, it is called a self-correction. To record a self-correction, first write the incorrect response(s), and when the child reads the word correctly, mark SC. Separate the incorrect response(s) and the SC with a vertical line. Draw a line under the incorrect response(s) and the SC, and write the correct word below the line.

| Text | Student Says | How to Record |
|------|-------------|---------------|
| **I need my coat.** | I need my jacket, coat. | **EXAMPLE 1:** Self-correction with one incorrect response<br><br>✓ ✓ ✓ $\frac{\text{jacket}}{\text{coat}}$ \| SC |
| | I need my jacket, sweater, coat. | **EXAMPLE 2:** Self-correction with more than one incorrect response<br><br>✓ ✓ ✓ $\frac{\text{jacket}}{\text{coat}}$ \| sweater \| SC |

## Adding and Skipping Words

### Insertion

When a child adds a word, it is called an insertion. Record it by writing the child's insertion, drawing a line under it, and adding a dash below the line to indicate that the word is not in the text.

| Text | Student Says | How to Record |
|------|-------------|---------------|
| **"Yes, it is!" said Mom.** | Yes, it is, said my mom. | ✓ ✓ ✓ ✓ $\frac{\text{my}}{-}$ ✓ |

### Omission

When a child skips a word, it is called an omission. Record it by writing a dash to represent the omitted word, draw a line under it, and write the word as it appears in the text below the line.

| Text | Student Says | How to Record |
|------|-------------|---------------|
| **"Now we can go outside,"** | Now we can go, | ✓ ✓ ✓ ✓ $\frac{-}{\text{outside}}$ |
| **said Mom and Dad.** | said Mom and Dad. | ✓ ✓ ✓ ✓ |

# Repetitions and Rereadings

## Repetition of a Correct Response

When a child repeats the word from the text, use a check mark to indicate the child read the word correctly, and then write R to indicate he or she repeated it. Don't put a space between the check mark and the R. You want the repeated word to be obvious.

| Text | Student Says | How to Record |
|---|---|---|
| **It is a rainy day.** | It is a rainy, rainy day. | ✓ ✓ ✓ ✓R ✓ |

## Repetition of a Substitution

When a child repeats a substitution, first record the word read incorrectly, and then write an R to indicate that the substitution has been repeated. Separate the substitution and R with a vertical line. Draw a line under the substitution and R, and write the word as it appears in the text below the line.

| Text | Student Says | How to Record |
|---|---|---|
| **I need my coat.** | I need my jacket, jacket. | ✓ ✓ ✓ $\frac{\text{jacket} \mid \text{R}}{\text{coat} \mid}$ |

## Multiple Repetitions of a Correct Response

When a child repeats the word from the text, use a check mark to indicate the child read the word correctly, and write R to indicate that he or she repeated it. Number the R to note how many times the child repeated the word.

| Text | Student Says | How to Record |
|---|---|---|
| **It is a rainy day.** | It is a rainy, rainy, rainy day. | ✓ ✓ ✓ ✓R$_2$ ✓ |

## Multiple Repetitions of a Substitution

When a child repeats a substitution, first record the word he or she read incorrectly, write an R to indicate that the substitution has been repeated, and separate the substitution and R with a vertical line. Number the R to note how many times the child repeated the substitution. Draw a line under the substitution and R, and write the word as it appears in the text below the line.

| Text | Student Says | How to Record |
| --- | --- | --- |
| I need my coat. | I need my jacket, jacket, jacket. | ✓ ✓ ✓ $\dfrac{\text{jacket}}{\text{coat}}$ R$_2$ |

## Repetition of More Than One Word

When a child repeats more than one word, whether he or she goes back to the beginning of the sentence, a phrase, or a couple of words, write an R. Then draw an arrow to indicate the point at which the child returned and began rereading.

| Text | Student Says | How to Record |
| --- | --- | --- |
| It is a rainy day. | It is a it is a rainy day. | ↓✓ ✓ ✓ R ✓ ✓ |

## Repetition of More Than One Word With a Self-Correction on the Rereading

When a child substitutes a word and then rereads, first record the substitution, write an R, and separate the substitution and R with a vertical line. Then draw an arrow to indicate the point at which the child returned and began rereading. If the child self-corrects after the rereading, draw another vertical line and mark SC, as shown in Example 1. If the child self-corrects while rereading, indicate where he or she self-corrected by dropping a line and recording SC, as shown in Example 2.

| Text | Student Says | How to Record |
| --- | --- | --- |
| I need my coat. | | **EXAMPLE 1:** SC after rereading |
| Is it in the closet? | | |
| | I need my coat. | ✓ ✓ ✓ ✓ |
| | Is it in my is it in the closet? | ↓✓ ✓ ✓ $\dfrac{\text{my}}{\text{the}}$ R ǀ SC ✓ |
| | | **EXAMPLE 2:** SC during rereading |
| | I need my coat. | ✓ ✓ ✓ ✓ |
| | Is it in my closet? Is it in the closet? | ↓✓ ✓ ✓ $\dfrac{\text{my}}{\text{the}}$ ǀ SC ✓ R |

# Word Analysis and Multiple Attempts

## Decoding Attempt

When a child uses letter sounds to analyze a word, indicate those sounds using lowercase letters. Use dashes to indicate how the child used initial letter, blends or digraphs, onset and rime, syllables, or other sound units when decoding.

| Text | Student Says | How to Record |
|---|---|---|
| **I need my hat.**<br><br>**Is it on the shelf?** | I need my h-at/hat.<br><br>Is it on the sh-shelf? | ✓ ✓ ✓ $\frac{\text{h-at ✓}}{\text{hat}}$<br><br>✓ ✓ ✓ ✓ sh ✓ |

## Multiple Decoding Attempts

When a child makes multiple attempts using sounds to analyze a word, separate each attempt with a vertical line to indicate the child's decoding efforts.

| Text | Student Says | How to Record |
|---|---|---|
| **In the morning,**<br>**we went**<br>**to look for berries.** | In the m – or – ing \| moring, mor – n – ing \| morning we went to look for berries. | ✓✓ $\frac{\text{m-or-ing}}{\text{morning}}$\|$\frac{\text{moring}}{\text{ }}$\|$\frac{\text{mor-n-ing}}{\text{ }}$\| ✓<br><br>✓ ✓<br>✓ ✓ ✓ ✓ |

## Spelling Out a Word

When a child spells a word out loud, record each letter in the word using uppercase letters.

| Text | Student Says | How to Record |
|---|---|---|
| **It is a rainy day.** | It is a rainy D-A-Y day. | ✓ ✓ ✓ ✓ $\frac{\text{D-A-Y ✓}}{\text{day}}$ |

## Requests for Help or No Action

### *Appeal*

When a child asks for help, it is called an appeal. Record the appeal by writing an A, drawing a line under it, and writing the challenging word below the line. After the child appeals, wait, especially if he or she appears to be actively working to solve the word. If the child proceeds to read the word correctly, use a check mark to record the accurate reading, as shown in Example 1. If, however, the child substitutes a word and keeps reading, draw a vertical line and record the substitution, as shown in Example 2.

| Text | Student Says | How to Record |
|---|---|---|
| **I need my boots.** | | **EXAMPLE 1:** Appeal followed by a correct response |
| **Are they by the door?** | | |
| **"Yes, they are!" said Dad.** | I need my boots. | ✓ ✓ ✓ ✓ |
| | Are | ✓ $\frac{A}{they}$ \| ✓ ✓ ✓ |
| | S: "I don't know that word." | |
| | T: (says nothing and waits) | ✓ ✓ ✓ ✓ ✓ |
| | S: they by the door? | |
| | Yes, they are, said Dad. | |
| | | **EXAMPLE 2:** Appeal followed by a substitution |
| | I need my boots. | ✓ ✓ ✓ ✓ |
| | Are | ✓ $\frac{A}{they}$ \| them ✓ ✓ ✓ |
| | S: "I don't know that word." | |
| | T: (says nothing and waits) | ✓ ✓ ✓ ✓ ✓ |
| | S: them by the door? | |
| | Yes, they are, said Dad. | |

## Told

Children often know when they have made an error and, after making a substitution, will appeal for help. When that happens, tell the child the word, write A above the line to indicate the appeal, and write T below the line to indicate the Told. You can give a Told when the child makes an appeal and refuses to continue reading. When that occurs, and you have offered the necessary wait time, tell the word to the child, and write a T below the line to indicate the Told. This will likely keep the child moving along. Avoid doing it too frequently, so that the child doesn't become dependent on you and misses the opportunity to engage in problem solving.

| Text | Student Says | How to Record |
|---|---|---|
| **I need my boots.** | I need my boots. | ✓ ✓ ✓ ✓ |
| **Are they by the door?** | Are the | ✓  $\dfrac{\text{the } |A|}{\text{they} \quad |T}$  ✓ ✓ ✓ |
| **"Yes, they are!" said Dad.** | S: "I don't know that word." | |
| | T: (waits, gives a Told *they*) | ✓ ✓ ✓ ✓ ✓ |
| | S: by the door? | |
| | Yes, they are, said Dad. | |

## You Try It

When the child takes no action, and you have offered the appropriate wait time, he or she may ask for help. At that point, and only at that point, you can say, "You try it." Remember, what the text says and what you say goes below the line, so first record the child's appeal above the line with an A, and then write a Y below the line to indicate that you prompted the child to try it. After waiting, if the child makes no attempt, tell the child the word and write a T below the line, as shown in Example 1 on the next page. If the child reads the word correctly, put a check mark above the line, as shown in Example 2. If the child substitutes a word and keeps reading, record the substitution, as shown in Example 3. Don't forget to use vertical lines to separate each attempt or action. These are just a few examples of the complex behaviors you may witness as the child interacts with text.

| Text | Student Says | How to Record |
|---|---|---|
| **I need my boots.**<br><br>**Are they by the door?**<br><br>**"Yes, they are!" said Dad.** | | **EXAMPLE 1:** Appeal, "You try it," No attempt, Told |
| | I need my boots. | ✓ ✓ ✓ ✓ |
| | Are | ✓   $\dfrac{\text{A} \mid \ \mid}{\text{they} \mid \text{Y} \mid \text{T}}$   ✓ ✓ ✓ |
| | S: "I don't know that word." | |
| | T: Waits, then says, "You try it." | ✓ ✓ ✓ ✓ ✓ |
| | The student takes no action, so the teacher gives a Told on *they*. | |
| | S: by the door? | |
| | Yes, they are, said Dad. | |
| | | **EXAMPLE 2:** Appeal, "You try it," Correct Response |
| | I need my boots. | ✓ ✓ ✓ ✓ |
| | Are | ✓   $\dfrac{\ \mid \text{A} \mid \ \mid}{\text{they} \mid \ \mid \text{Y} \mid}$ ✓   ✓ ✓ ✓ |
| | S: "I don't know that word." | |
| | T: Waits, then says, "You try it." | ✓ ✓ ✓ ✓ ✓ |
| | S: they by the door? | |
| | Yes, they are, said Dad. | |
| | | **EXAMPLE 3:** Appeal, "You try it," Substitution |
| | I need my boots. | ✓ ✓ ✓ ✓ |
| | Are | ✓   $\dfrac{\ \mid \text{A} \mid \ \mid \text{boots}}{\text{they} \mid \ \mid \text{Y} \mid}$ ✓ ✓ ✓ |
| | S: "I don't know that word." | |
| | T: Waits, then says, "You try it." | ✓ ✓ ✓ ✓ ✓ |
| | S: boots by the door? | |
| | Yes, they are, said Dad. | |

# FROM PRACTICE TO PROFICIENCY

Taking a running record may seem easy, but becoming proficient at it takes practice. After years of taking running records every day, we are still honing our skills. We regularly check on ourselves to make sure we are recording children's every action and behavior. If you are already comfortable with running records, one way to check yourself is to audio- or video-record a child's reading and use it to review your coding. When we do this, we are often amazed at the little things we miss. While this may seem tedious, accurately capturing a child's actions and behaviors provides important insights about his or her reading.

One of our favorite mantras is "practice leads to proficiency," so here's an opportunity for you to take a running record. When you're finished, check your work against the answer key at the end of the chapter.

| Text | Student Says | Practice Recording |
|---|---|---|
|  It is a rainy day. 2 | It is a r- rainy day. | |
|  I need my coat. Is it in the closet? "Yes, it is!" said Mom. 3 | I need a coat. <br><br> Is it in the closet? <br><br> in the closet? <br><br> Yes, it is! said Mother. | |

| Text | Student Says | Practice Recording |
|---|---|---|

I need my hat.

Is it in the shelf?

Is it on the shelf?

Yes, it is! said D-ad, Dad.

I need my umbrella.

Is it on the hook?

Yes, it is! said Mother,

Mom.

I need my boots.

Are they by the front door?

Yes, they are! said Dad.

| Text | Student Says | Practice Recording |
|---|---|---|
|  "Now we can go outside," said Mom and Dad. 7 | Now, now we can go, said Mom and Dad. | |
|  It is not a rainy day. It is a rainbow day! 8 | It is N-O-T, not a rainy day. It is a rainbow day! | |

An answer key is provided at the end of the chapter.

## CLOSING THOUGHT

While it may not take the 10,000 hours that Malcolm Gladwell suggests in *Outliers*, practicing will improve your ability to take a running record in the classroom quickly and accurately. Therefore, in addition to the information in this chapter, we have also created a quick reference guide on standard coding to support you. See Appendix A, pages 232–234, and scholastic.com/ResourcesNSFRR. In our work with teachers, we have found that having this guide available when taking a running record answers many questions on the spot and builds proficiency.

**Answer key to the practice activity on pages 44–46**

| Text | Student Says | Correct Recording |
|---|---|---|
|  It is a rainy day. 2 | It is a r- rainy day. | ✓ ✓ ✓ r-✓ ✓ |

| | Student Says | Correct Recording |
|---|---|---|
| I need my coat. Is it in the closet? "Yes, it is!" said Mom. 3 | I need a coat. | ✓ ✓ $\frac{a}{my}$ ✓ |
| | Is it in the closet? | ✓ ✓✓̌ ✓ ✓R |
| | in the closet? | |
| | Yes, it is! said Mother. | ✓ ✓ ✓ ✓ $\frac{Mother}{Mom}$ |

| | Student Says | Correct Recording |
|---|---|---|
| I need my hat. Is it on the shelf? "Yes, it is!" said Dad. 4 | I need my hat. | ✓ ✓ ✓ ✓ |
| | Is it in the shelf? | ✓ ✓ $\frac{in}{on}$ SC ✓ ✓R |
| | Is it on the shelf? | |
| | Yes, it is! said D-ad, Dad. | ✓ ✓ ✓ ✓ $\frac{D\text{-}ad✓}{Dad}$ |

| Text | Student Says | Correct Recording |
|------|-------------|-------------------|
|  I need my umbrella. Is it on the hook? "Yes, it is!" said Mom. | I need my umbrella. | ✓ ✓ ✓ ✓ |
| | Is it on the hook? | ✓ ✓ ✓ ✓ ✓ |
| | Yes, it is! said Mother, Mom. | ✓ ✓ ✓ ✓ ✓ Mother\|SC ⟋ Mom \| |
|  I need my boots. Are they by the door? "Yes, they are!" said Dad. | I need my boots. | ✓ ✓ ✓ ✓ |
| | Are they by the front door? | ✓ ✓ ✓ ✓ front ✓ ⟋ - |
| | Yes, they are! said Dad. | ✓ ✓ ✓ ✓ ✓ |
| "Now we can go outside," said Mom and Dad. | Now, now we can go, | ✓R ✓ ✓ ✓ - ⟋ outside |
| | said Mom and Dad. | ✓ ✓ ✓ ✓ |

| Text | Student Says | Correct Recording |
|---|---|---|
| It is not a rainy day.<br>It is a rainbow day!<br><br>8 | It is N-O-T, not a rainy day. | ✓ ✓ <u>N-O-T✓</u> ✓ ✓ ✓<br>     not |
| | It is a rainbow day! | ✓ ✓ ✓ ✓ ✓ |

# CHAPTER 4

# Calculating Accuracy and Self-Correction Rates

In this chapter, we examine more closely what constitutes an error and a self-correction, and how to calculate accuracy and self-correction rates. We also explain what accuracy and self-correction rates mean and their implications for teaching.

Consider the running record on the next page. The child made five errors on a text of 81 words and self-corrected twice. That means her accuracy rate is 94 percent and the self-correction rate is 1:4. A 1:4 self-correction rate indicates she corrected one out of every four errors. If this child was in your class, what would you be thinking? Examine the running record and then use these guiding questions to write your thoughts in the space at the end of the chart.

- How well do you think the child read this text?
- Do you think the child should be given a text at a higher level?
- The child corrected one out of every four errors. Is the self-correction rate of 1:4 a problem?

| Text | Correct Recording | Errors | Self-Corrections |
|---|---|---|---|
|   It is a rainy day.  2 | ✓ ✓ ✓  r-✓  ✓ | | |
|   I need my coat.  Is it in the closet?  "Yes, it is!" said Mom.  3 | ✓ ✓ $\underline{\substack{a \\ my}}$ ✓  ✓ ✓ ✓ ✓ ✓ R  ✓ ✓ ✓ ✓ $\underline{\substack{Mother \\ Mom}}$ | 1  1 | |
|   I need my hat.  Is it on the shelf?  "Yes, it is!" said Dad.  4 | ✓ ✓ ✓ ✓  ✓ ✓ $\underline{\substack{in \\ on}}$ \| SC ✓ ✓R  ✓ ✓ ✓ ✓ $\underline{\substack{D-ad✓ \\ Dad}}$ | 1 | |

| Text | Correct Recording | Errors | Self-Corrections |
|---|---|---|---|
| <br>I need my umbrella.<br>Is it on the hook?<br>"Yes, it is!" said Mom. | ✓ ✓ ✓ ✓<br><br>✓ ✓ ✓ ✓ ✓<br><br>✓ ✓ ✓ ✓ ✓ $\frac{\text{Mother}}{\text{Mom}}$ │ SC | | 1 |
| <br>I need my boots.<br>Are they by the door?<br>"Yes, they are!" said Dad. | ✓ ✓ ✓ ✓<br><br>✓ ✓ ✓ ✓ $\frac{\text{front}}{-}$ ✓<br><br>✓ ✓ ✓ ✓ ✓ | 1 | |
| <br>"Now we can go outside,"<br>said Mom and Dad. | ✓R ✓ ✓ ✓ $\frac{-}{\text{outside}}$<br><br>✓ ✓ ✓ ✓ | 1 | |

| Text | Correct Recording | Errors | Self-Corrections |
|------|-------------------|--------|------------------|

It is not a rainy day.
It is a rainbow day!

8

✓ ✓  $\dfrac{\text{N-O-T} \mid \text{A} \mid}{\text{not} \mid\ \ \mid \text{T}}$  ✓ ✓ ✓     1

✓ ✓ ✓ ✓ ✓

## Your Thoughts

### Guiding Questions

- How well do you think the child read this text?
- Do you think the child should be given a text at a higher level?
- The child corrected one out of every four errors. Is the self-correction rate of 1:4 a problem?

## Our Thoughts

An accuracy rate of 94 percent indicates the text is at the child's instructional level. While this is at the upper end of the instructional range, we would hesitate to move the child to a higher text level given her self-correction rate of 1:4, which is positive, but approaching problematic. It would be beneficial to examine multiple running records to see if high self-correction rates are a pattern. If the child's other self-correction rates are in an acceptable range, the 1:4 may be a reflection of this particular text or the way in which it was introduced. As we learned from Ed Young's *Seven Blind Mice* about the disadvantages of having partial information, accuracy and self-correction rates provide only partial information and, therefore, give us a limited view of the child's processing. In the next chapter, we will discuss how to analyze error and self-correction behavior to give us a more complete picture of a child's processing.

# AN ERROR: WHAT IT IS AND WHAT IT ISN'T

As discussed in Chapter 3, there are many ways a child can deviate from the words in a text. They may make a substitution, an omission, or an insertion—and for the purposes of running records, each one is considered an error. But sometimes things are not always so clear-cut. It can be difficult to decide if something the child has done should be considered an error. In this section, we explain common confusions.

## Multiple Attempts

Teachers often question how to score an error when a child makes multiple attempts at a word, especially when the correct response is embedded in the attempts. Keep in mind, when taking a running record, it is the child's *final* attempt that determines whether it is an error.

### Running Record Scoring Rules: Scoring an Error on Multiple Attempts

The child says the word *jacket* for *coat* and then says *coat*, which is a self-correction (SC), and finally says *sweater*. Even though the child self-corrected during one of the attempts, the final word, *sweater*, was incorrect. The entire episode is scored as one error.

$$\frac{jacket \mid SC \mid sweater}{coat \mid \quad \mid}$$

Similarly, if the child reads the word correctly on the first attempt and then in subsequent attempts reads it incorrectly, it is scored as an error—for example, if the child says *coat*, then says *jacket*, and then says *sweater*.

$$\frac{\checkmark \mid jacket \mid sweater}{\mid coat \mid}$$

## Proper Nouns

Another confusion involves scoring proper nouns. If a child repeatedly substitutes a character's name for the one in the text, you should record the substitution each time, but only as an error the first time. For example, if the character's name in a text is Katie, and the child repeatedly substitutes *Kate*, you would record each time the child uses *Kate*, but consider only the first attempt an error.

When the character's name also represents their family role, such as *Mother* or *Dad*, the name is considered a proper noun and is treated as such. So if the child repeatedly says *Mom* for *Mother* or *Mama Bear* for *Mother Bear* while reading, count it as one error the first time the child makes it.

Further, if you tell the child the name (e.g., *Katie* or *Mother*) during the reading, record it as a Told and score it as an error. If you give the child a Told later in the reading on the same proper noun, only score it as an error the first time the child makes it.

## Repeated Errors

When a child repeats an error on a word that is *not* a proper noun—for example, reads *comes* for *came*, or *runs* for *ran*—record it as an error every time he or she makes it.

## Mispronunciations

Mispronunciations, or issues with articulation, such as *pasghetti* for *spaghetti* or *fum* for *thumb*, are not considered reading errors, but rather speech errors that will most likely be corrected as the child's speech matures. Do not score them as reading errors.

Sometimes the mispronunciation is related to a child's dialect. For example, the child reads *aks* for the word *ask*. In other cases, a child may overgeneralize the *-ed* ending and read, for example, *look-did* for *looked*. Again, these are not reading errors. Dialect-related mispronunciations need to be addressed instructionally but should not be tallied as errors (see Chapter 10 for more information).

## Contractions

When a child reads a contraction for the two words that make up the contraction (e.g., *did not* for *didn't*), count it as only one error. Likewise, when he or she reads a contraction for the two words, it also counts as one error (e.g., *hasn't* for *has not*).

The chart on the next page highlights the most frequent types of errors and confusions about errors.

| An Error | | Not an Error | |
|---|---|---|---|
| Substitution | jacket / coat | Self-correction | jacket \|SC / coat \| |
| Insertion | my / - | Repetition on a correct response | ✓R |
| Omission | - / outside | Decoding | h-at✓ / hat |
| Repetition on a substitution (only counts as one error regardless of how many times the substitution is repeated) | jacket \|R₂ / coat \| | Multiple decoding attempts that result in a correct response | mor-ing \| morn-ing \| ✓ / morning \| \| |
| Spelling out a word without saying the correct word | D-A-Y / day | Spelling out a word that results in saying the correct word | D-A-Y ✓ / day |
| Told | ___\|A\|___ / coat \| \|T | | |

*For a complete explanation of student behaviors and how they are scored, see Recording and Scoring Student Behaviors in Appendix A, pages 232–234, and at scholastic.com/ResourcesNSFRR.*

**Running Record Scoring Rules:
Scoring Episodes Involving "Tolds"**

A child says the word *jacket* for *coat* and then appeals for help. The teacher waits and then gives the word *coat*. If the child says the correct word after the Told, it is not a self-correction because the child has actually repeated the teacher's Told, so it should be recorded as an error. But be sure to note that the child repeated the word so that you have an accurate record of how he or she worked on and processed text.

For example:

$$\frac{\text{jacket} \mid A \mid \quad \text{coat}}{\text{coat} \quad \mid \quad \mid T \mid}$$

Sometimes, after the teacher gives a child a Told, the child will reread at the phrase or sentence level to regain meaning. While that may be a productive thing to do, you should still record it as an error because the teacher gave a Told.

For example:

$$\checkmark\checkmark\checkmark \; \frac{\text{jacket} \mid A \mid \quad \text{coat} \mid R}{\text{coat} \quad \mid \quad \mid T \mid \qquad \mid}$$

# A SELF-CORRECTION:
# WHAT IT IS AND WHAT IT ISN'T

When a child deviates from a word in the text and then reads the word correctly, it is called a self-correction. *A self-correction is not counted as an error!*

# FROM PRACTICE TO PROFICIENCY

Use the book *Hang on Tight!* by C.C. Bates and Maryann McBride (Level E) to practice tallying errors and self-corrections. When you're finished, check your work against the answer key at the end of the chapter. And see Recording and Scoring Student Behaviors, a complete reference guide for what should be counted as an error or self-correction, in Appendix A, pages 232–234, and at scholastic.com/ResourcesNSFRR.

| Text | Running Record | Errors | Self-Correction |
|---|---|---|---|
| 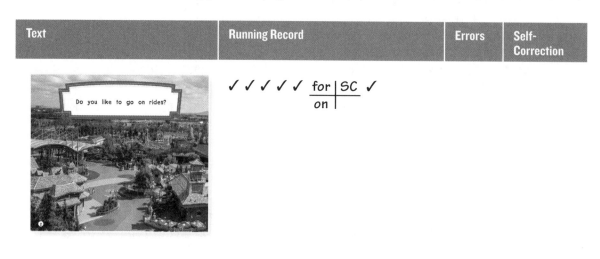<br>Do you like to go on rides? | ✓ ✓ ✓ ✓ ✓ for \| SC ✓<br>               on \| | | |
| <br>Rides move in lots of ways.<br>**Hang on tight!** | ✓ m✓ ✓ ✓ ✓ w-ay \| way<br>   move       ways \|<br><br>✓ ✓ ✓ | | |

| Text | Running Record | Errors | Self-Correction |
|---|---|---|---|

✓ ✓ ✓ R

✓ ✓ ✓ ✓

✓ ✓ ✓ ✓ ✓ ✓

✓ ✓ ✓

$\dfrac{\text{hold}}{\text{hang}}$ ✓ ✓

 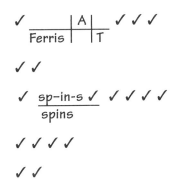

✓ $\dfrac{\quad}{\text{Ferris}}$ | A | T ✓ ✓ ✓

✓ ✓

✓ $\dfrac{\text{sp-in-s}}{\text{spins}}$ ✓ ✓ ✓ ✓ ✓

✓ ✓ ✓ ✓

✓ ✓

✓ ✓ ✓

| Text | Running Record | Errors | Self-Correction |
|---|---|---|---|

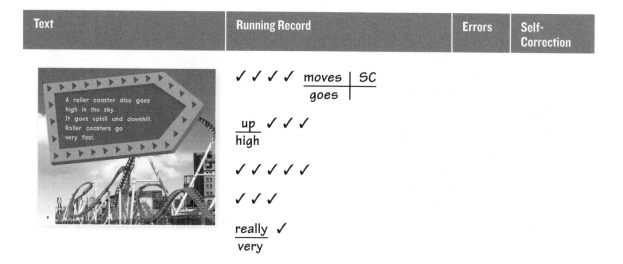

A roller coaster also goes high in the sky. It goes uphill and downhill. Roller coasters go very fast.

✓ ✓ ✓ ✓ $\dfrac{\text{moves}}{\text{goes}}$ | SC

$\dfrac{\text{up}}{\text{high}}$ ✓ ✓ ✓

✓ ✓ ✓ ✓ ✓

✓ ✓ ✓

$\dfrac{\text{really}}{\text{very}}$ ✓

An answer key is provided at the end of the chapter.

## CALCULATING ACCURACY AND SELF-CORRECTION RATES

Once you have tallied the number of errors and self-corrections on a running record, use the information to calculate the reader's accuracy and self-correction rates.

### Accuracy Rate

A child's accuracy rate is the percentage of words he or she reads correctly. First, find the total number of words in a text, often referred to as running words (RW). Most publishers include this information on the inside cover or at the end of the book. If the information is not available, count the words and record the total on the book. Next, subtract the number of errors (E) from the running words to determine the number of words read accurately (RW - E). Divide the number of words read accurately by the total number of words and multiply by 100 to obtain a percentage—or, the child's accuracy rate.

Formula for Accuracy Rate:

$$\dfrac{\text{RW} - \text{E}}{\text{RW}} \times 100 = \text{Accuracy Rate (percentage)}$$

| Running Words | # of Errors | Formula | Accuracy Rate |
|---|---|---|---|
| 65 | 5 | $65 - 5 = \dfrac{60}{65} = .923 \times 100 = 92\%$ | 92% |
| 72 | 4 | Your Turn | Your Turn |

An answer key is provided at the end of the chapter.

## *What Does Accuracy Rate Indicate?*

The accuracy rate allows you to gauge how difficult the reading of a text was for a child. However, it's important to keep in mind that a running record is much more than a tool for computing child's accuracy. Running records provide teachers with instructional insights on how different texts can provide unique teaching and learning opportunities in individual, small-group, and whole-class contexts. Too often, teachers use accuracy rate to assign a text level and overlook the complete record, which contains pertinent information about the child's processing.

While we advocate for using a complete record, the accuracy rate can indicate how difficult or easy a text level is for the reader. For example, multiple running records that yield an accuracy rate at a child's independent level could imply the need for a higher-level text to increase teaching and learning opportunities. The same could be said about lowering the level if multiple running records are at a child's frustration level. Reading texts that repeatedly fall below 90 percent could indicate the text level is too difficult, and the child likely needs a text that will allow for more control.

The chart below links accuracy rates and instructional implications.

| Accuracy Rate | Instructional Implications |
|---|---|
| 95–100 % | Text read at this rate can be read with little or no instructional assistance. It is appropriate for independent reading and provides practice in building fluency and comprehension. |
| 90–94 % | Text read at this rate provides enough challenge to support problem solving. It is appropriate for small-group instruction and should be read with teacher scaffolding. The teacher usually provides a book introduction, prompts the student at points of difficulty, and leads a discussion to facilitate the comprehension of the text. |
| < 90 % | Text read at this rate may be too difficult for the child to read on his own. When text is too hard, children can feel frustrated and might abandon the reading or engage in "pretend" reading. Texts that are too difficult for children to read independently are definitely appropriate for read-alouds or shared reading. Using these texts for read-alouds and shared reading builds vocabulary, conceptual knowledge, and familiarity with complex language and literary structures. |

# Self-Correction Rate

A child's self-correction rate is a ratio that is sometimes tricky to calculate and understand. So let's begin with an example. When computing a self-correction rate, it is important to remember that a self-correction is an error that the child has corrected. Therefore, the rate is technically a ratio that expresses the number of self-corrections in relation to the number of errors, plus the errors that were self-corrected (E+SC). If a child's first attempts resulted in 18 errors (E+SC), but six were corrected, the child's SC rate is 6/18, a ratio 1:3.

Formula for Self-Correction Rate:

$$\frac{SC}{E + SC} = \textbf{Self-Correction Rate (ratio)}$$

Let's apply the above example (6 SC, 12 E) to the formula:

$$\frac{6}{12 + 6} = \frac{6}{18} = \frac{1}{3} = \textbf{1:3}$$

When calculating a self-correction rate, any part of a whole number is rounded to the next whole number, regardless of the mathematical rules that apply to rounding numbers. For example, 1/3.33 would be expressed as 1:4. The only time a self-correction rate is computed as 1:1 is when a child has self-corrected every error.

| # of Self-Corrections | # of Errors | Formula | Self-Correction Rate |
|---|---|---|---|
| 6 | 5 | $\frac{6}{5 + 6} = \frac{6}{11} = \frac{1}{1.83}$ | **1:2** This means for every 2 opportunities, the child corrected 1 time. |
| 3 | 7 | $\frac{3}{7 + 3} = \frac{3}{10} = \frac{1}{3.33}$ | **1:4** This means for every 4 opportunities, the child corrected 1 time. |
| 0 | 5 | $\frac{0}{5 + 0} = \frac{0}{5}$ | **0:5** This means for every 5 opportunities, the child corrected 0 times. |
| 2 | 6 | Your Turn | Your Turn |

An answer key is provided at the end of the chapter.

# FROM PRACTICE TO PROFICIENCY

Now let's put it all together and practice calculating both the accuracy rate and self-correction rate. You'll find an answer key at the end of the chapter.

| Running Words | # of Errors | # of Self-Corrections | Accuracy Rate | Self-Correction Rate |
|---|---|---|---|---|
| 100 | 6 | 4 | | |
| 83 | 2 | 0 | | |
| 140 | 8 | 9 | | |
| 120 | 14 | 7 | | |
| 96 | 6 | 3 | | |
| 72 | 7 | 1 | | |
| 54 | 4 | 8 | | |

An answer key is provided at the end of the chapter.

### What Does Self-Correction Rate Indicate?

If a child is not engaging in self-correcting behavior based on your review of multiple running records, it is a reflection on our teaching. We must teach children to check on themselves and problem-solve to self-correct.

When a child's self-correction rate is 1:2 or 1:3, it indicates that she is noticing and fixing many errors. She is checking on herself and problem solving while reading. When the self-correction rate is 1:5 or higher, it indicates that the child is ignoring many reading errors. Self-corrections have a high tutorial value because they were self-initiated and reinforce the child's independent reading behaviors. A child with a high self-correction rate is missing out on the opportunity to monitor her reading, problem-solve, and practice the skills to become a successful reader. There are many reasons a child may be ignoring errors. These are discussed in Chapter 7.

The chart below provides a guide for interpreting self-correction rates by linking rate, behavior, and instructional implications.

| Interpreting Self-Correction Rates | | |
|---|---|---|
| **Self-Correction Rate** | **Self-Correcting Behavior** | **Instructional Implications** |
| 1:1 – 1:4 | Positive | Self-correction rates in this range show the child is noticing and actively problem-solving to correct errors. This is also an indication of successful teaching and learning. |
| > 1:5 | Problematic | Self-correction rates in this range show the child is not noticing errors and therefore is not engaging in problem solving that would lead to self-correction. This may be an indication that the child does not know what to do. The teacher should make instructional adjustments. |

## CLOSING THOUGHT

In the running record that opened the chapter, you will recall that the child made five errors on a text of 81 words and self-corrected twice. Her accuracy rate was 94 percent and her self-correction rate was 1:4. We asked you to make some initial assumptions about the child's reading. Given what you have learned from this chapter, how would you describe the reader now?

## Answer key to the practice activity on pages 58–60

| Text | Running Record | Errors | Self-Corrections |
|---|---|---|---|
| Do you like to go on rides? | ✓ ✓ ✓ ✓ ✓ $\frac{\text{for}}{\text{on}}$ \| SC ✓ | | 1 |
| Rides move in lots of ways. *Hang on tight!* | ✓ $\frac{\text{m✓}}{\text{move}}$ ✓ ✓ ✓ $\frac{\text{w-ay}}{\text{ways}}$ \| way <br> ✓ ✓ ✓ | 1 | |
| A merry-go-round goes in a big circle. The horses go up and down, up and down. *Hang on tight!* | ⌐✓ ✓ ✓┐R <br> ✓ ✓ ✓ ✓ <br> ✓ ✓ ✓ ✓ ✓ ✓ <br> ✓ ✓ ✓ <br> $\frac{\text{hold}}{\text{hang}}$ ✓ ✓ | 1 | |

| Text | Running Record | Errors | Self-Corrections |
|---|---|---|---|
| 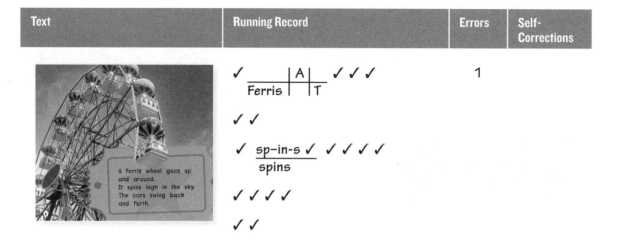 | ✓ — A ✓ ✓ ✓ <br> ‾‾‾‾‾  ‾‾ <br> Ferris  T <br><br> ✓ ✓ <br><br> ✓ sp–in–s ✓ ✓ ✓ ✓ <br>   ‾‾‾‾‾‾‾ <br>   spins <br><br> ✓ ✓ ✓ ✓ <br><br> ✓ ✓ | 1 | |
|  | ✓ ✓ ✓ | | |
| 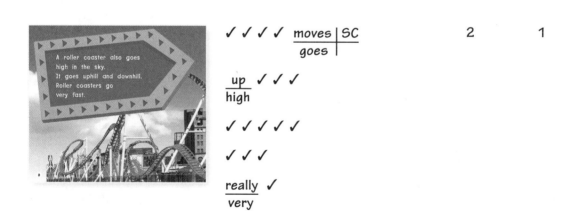 | ✓ ✓ ✓ ✓ moves \| SC <br>        ‾‾‾‾‾‾ <br>         goes \| <br><br> up ✓ ✓ ✓ <br> ‾‾‾ <br> high <br><br> ✓ ✓ ✓ ✓ ✓ <br><br> ✓ ✓ ✓ <br><br> really ✓ <br> ‾‾‾‾‾ <br> very | 2 | 1 |

## Answer key to the practice activity on page 60

| Running Words | # of Errors | Formula | Accuracy Rate |
|---|---|---|---|
| 72 | 4 | $72-4 = \dfrac{68}{72}$ = .944 X 100 = 94% | 94% |

## Answer key to the practice activity on page 62

| # of Self-Corrections | # of Errors | Formula | Self-Correction Rate |
|---|---|---|---|
| 2 | 6 | $\dfrac{2}{2+6} = \dfrac{2}{8} = \dfrac{1}{4}$ | 1:4 |

## Answer key to the practice activity on page 63

| Running Words | # of Errors | # of Self-Corrections | Accuracy Rate | Self-Correction Rate |
|---|---|---|---|---|
| 100 | 6 | 4 | 94% | 1:3 |
| 83 | 2 | 0 | 98% | 0:2 |
| 140 | 8 | 9 | 94% | 1:2 |
| 120 | 14 | 7 | 88% | 1:3 |
| 96 | 6 | 3 | 94% | 1:3 |
| 72 | 7 | 1 | 90% | 1:8 |
| 54 | 4 | 8 | 93% | 1:2 |

# CHAPTER 5

# Analyzing Errors and Self-Corrections

How many times do you take a running record, tally the errors and self-corrections, figure out the accuracy rate, ignore the self-correction rate, and file the information away? Determining accuracy rate and self-correction rate are important, but they are only one step in analyzing a running record. In this chapter, we challenge you to go further and take an in-depth look at the unique work each child is doing and what it reveals about his or her reading process.

## FROM PRACTICE TO PROFICIENCY

The chart on the following pages contains running records of three children reading the same book, *Miss Blake and the Pet Snake* by Myka-Lynne Sokoloff (Level G; running words: 301). Using what you learned in Chapter 4, tally the errors and self-corrections for each child and record the information in the chart on page 73. Use the number of running words, errors, and self-corrections to calculate accuracy and self-correction rates. Once you have completed the calculations, check your work against the answer key at the end of the chapter, and use the following guiding questions to reflect on how the children's work on the same text varies.

- What are the strengths and needs of each child?
- What do these records have in common?
- How would I use the information from the running records to plan instruction?

| Text | Running Record 1 | Running Record 2 | Running Record 3 |
|---|---|---|---|
| "Good morning, class," said Miss Blake. "Good morning," said the class. | ✓ ✓ ✓ ✓ ✓<br>✓ ✓ ✓ ✓ kids/class | ✓ ✓ ✓ ✓ ✓<br>✓ ✓ ✓ ✓ | ✓ ✓ ✓ ✓ ✓<br>✓ ✓ ✓ ✓ |
| "Can we get a class pet?" asked Dan. "I'm not sure," said Miss Blake. "Please, please, please!" said the children. | ✓ ✓ ✓ ✓ animal/pet ✓ ✓<br>✓ ✓ ✓ ✓ ✓<br>✓ ✓<br>✓ ✓ | ✓ ✓ do/get ✓ ✓ ✓ ✓<br>✓ ✓ ✓ ✓ ✓<br>✓ ✓ ✓<br>✓ ✓ ✓ | ✓ ✓ ✓ clash/class ✓ ✓ ✓<br>✓ never/not ✓ ✓ ✓<br>✓ ✓ ✓<br>✓ ✓ ✓ |
| "We can talk about it," said Miss Blake. "What animal would make a good class pet?" | ✓ ✓ ✓ ✓ ✓ ✓ ✓<br>✓ ✓ might/would ✓ ✓ ✓<br>✓ ✓ | ✓ ✓ ✓ ✓ ✓ ✓ ✓<br>✓ ✓ ✓ be/make ✓ ✓<br>✓ ✓ | ✓ ✓ ✓ ✓ ✓ ✓ ✓<br>✓ ✓ world/would ✓ ✓ ✓<br>✓ ✓ |
| Dan raised his hand. "Can we get a little dog?" asked Dan. "Dogs are too furry and they make me sneeze," said Miss Blake. "In fact, just the thought of them makes me sneeze. Ah-choo!" | ✓ ✓ ✓ ✓ ✓ ✓ ✓<br>✓ ✓ ✓<br>✓ ✓ ✓ hairy/furry ✓ ✓ ✓<br>✓ ✓ ✓ ✓ ✓<br>✓ ✓ ✓ ✓ ✓ ✓ ✓<br>✓ ✓ ✓ | ✓ ✓ ✓ legs/hand ✓ ✓ ✓<br>✓ ✓ ✓<br>✓ ✓ ✓ ✓ ✓ ✓<br>✓ ✓ ✓ ✓ ✓<br>✓ to/fact ✓ ✓ ✓ ✓<br>✓ ✓ laugh/sneeze ✓ | ✓ raced/raised ✓ ✓ ✓ ✓ ✓<br>✓ ✓ ✓<br>✓ ✓ ✓ ✓ ✓ ✓<br>✓ ✓ ✓ ✓ ✓<br>✓ ✓ ✓ ✓ think/thought ✓ ✓<br>✓ ✓ ✓ |

| Text | Running Record 1 | Running Record 2 | Running Record 3 |
|---|---|---|---|
| <br>"Can we get a pretty cat?" asked Cam.<br><br>"Ah-choo!" said Miss Blake.<br>"Cats are too furry.<br>And they make me sneeze." | ✓ ✓ ✓ ✓ ✓ ✓<br><br>✓ ✓ ✓<br><br>✓ ✓ ✓   messy ǀ R ǀ SC<br>         furry ǀ   ǀ<br><br>✓ ✓ ✓ ✓ | ✓ ✓ ✓ ✓ ✓ ✓<br><br>✓ ✓ ✓<br><br>✓ ✓ ✓<br><br>✓ ✓ ✓ ✓ | ✓ ✓ ✓ ✓ ✓ ✓ C-am✓<br>                    Cam<br><br>✓ ✓ ✓<br><br>✓ ✓ ✓   fur ǀ R ǀ SC<br>        furry ǀ   ǀ<br><br>✓ ✓ ✓ ✓ ✓ |
| <br>"Can we get a soft bunny?" asked Ben.<br><br>"Ah-choo!" said Miss Blake.<br>"Bunnies are too furry.<br>And they make me sneeze." | ✓ ✓ have ✓ ✓ rabbit ✓ ✓<br>     get       bunny<br><br>✓ ✓ ✓ ✓<br><br>✓ ✓ ✓ ✓<br><br>✓ ✓ ✓ ✓ | ✓ ✓ ✓ ✓ ✓ cookie ✓ ✓<br>             bunny<br><br>✓ ✓ ✓ ✓<br><br>✓ ✓ ✓ ✓<br><br>✓ ✓ ✓ ✓ | ✓ ✓ ✓ ✓ ✓ ✓ ✓<br><br>✓ ✓ ✓<br><br>✓ ✓ ✓ ✓<br><br>✓ ✓ ✓ ✓ |
| The children have more ideas.<br>Bob wants a hamster.<br>Meg wants a mouse.<br>Pat wants a pony. | ✓ ✓ ✓ ✓<br><br>✓ ✓ ✓<br><br>✓ ✓ ✓<br><br>✓ ✓ ✓ horse<br>        pony | ✓ ✓ ✓ ✓<br><br>✓ ✓ ✓ henhouse<br>        hamster<br><br>✓ ✓ ✓   prize<br>        mouse<br><br>✓ ✓ ✓ ice cream<br>         pony | ✓ ✓ ✓ ✓<br><br>✓ ✓ ✓ ham store<br>        hamster<br><br>✓ ✓ ✓   muse<br>        mouse<br><br>✓ ✓ ✓ ✓ |
| Miss Blake's nose got redder.<br>Her eyes did, too.<br>"Those will not do," she said sadly.<br>"Ah-choo! Ah-choo! Ah-choo!" | ✓ ✓ face ǀ SC ✓ ✓<br>     nose ǀ<br><br>✓ ✓ ✓<br><br>✓ ✓ ✓ ✓ ✓ ✓<br><br>✓ ✓ | ✓ ✓ ✓ ✓ ✓<br><br>✓ ✓ ✓ ✓<br><br>✓ ✓ ✓ ✓ ✓ ✓<br><br>✓ ✓ ✓ | ✓ ✓ ✓ ✓ reader ǀ SC<br>         redder ǀ<br><br>✓ ✓ ✓ ✓<br><br>These ✓ ✓ ✓ ✓ satly ǀ SC<br>Those         sadly ǀ<br><br>✓ ✓ ✓ |

| Text | Running Record 1 | Running Record 2 | Running Record 3 |
|---|---|---|---|
| Then Jen raised her hand. "I have a pet snake that needs a new home," she said.<br><br>"Oh?" said Miss Blake. "I'm not sure about a snake."<br><br>10 | They\|SC ✓✓✓✓✓✓<br>Then\|<br>✓✓✓✓✓✓<br>✓✓<br>✓✓✓✓✓✓<br>✓✓✓ | ✓✓✓✓✓✓<br>✓✓✓✓✓✓<br>✓✓<br>✓✓✓✓✓✓<br>✓✓ snack\|SC<br>    snake\| | They\|SC ✓✓✓✓✓✓<br>Then\|<br>✓✓✓✓✓✓<br>✓✓<br>✓✓✓✓✓✓<br>a-b-out ✓✓✓<br>  about |
| "A pet snake can help us learn our letters," said Cam.<br><br>"It can scare the lunch ladies, too!" said Dan.<br><br>"That is not nice, Dan." said Miss Blake.<br><br>11 | ✓✓✓✓✓✓ teach\|SC ✓<br>      learn\|<br>✓✓✓<br>✓✓ sc-✓ ✓✓✓✓<br>  scare<br>✓✓<br>✓✓✓✓✓<br>✓✓✓ | ✓✓✓✓✓✓✓<br>school\|SC ✓✓<br>letters\|<br>✓✓✓✓✓✓<br>✓✓<br>✓✓✓ big\|SC ✓<br>    nice\|<br>✓✓✓ | ✓✓✓✓✓✓ lean\|SC ✓<br>     learn\|<br>✓✓✓<br>✓✓ sc-✓ ✓✓✓✓<br>  scare<br>✓✓<br>✓✓✓✓✓<br>✓✓✓ |
| "A pet snake does not have fur," said Pat.<br><br>"Okay, we will try it," says Miss Blake.<br><br>12 | ✓✓✓✓✓ skin<br>     fur<br>✓✓<br>✓✓✓✓✓✓✓ | ✓✓✓✓✓✓<br>✓✓<br>✓✓✓✓✓✓✓ | ✓✓✓✓✓✓<br>✓✓<br>✓✓✓✓✓✓✓ |
| The snake came the next day.<br>It did not help with letters.<br>It did not scare the lunch ladies.<br><br>13 | ✓✓✓✓✓<br>✓✓✓ do\|SC ✓✓<br>   help\|<br>✓✓✓✓✓✓ | ✓✓✓✓✓ time<br>     day<br>✓✓✓✓✓✓<br>✓✓✓✓✓✓✓ | ✓✓✓✓✓<br>✓✓✓✓✓✓<br>✓✓✓✓✓✓✓ |

| Text | Running Record 1 | Running Record 2 | Running Record 3 |
|---|---|---|---|
| But the smoke did do a few fun things. It sat on laps. It gave nice hugs. | ✓ ✓ ✓ ✓ ✓ ✓ ✓ <br><br> ✓ ✓ ✓ ✓ <br><br> ✓ ✓ ✓ ✓ | And\|SC ✓ ✓ ✓ ✓ ✓ ✓ ✓<br>But\| <br><br> ✓ ✓ ✓ ✓ <br><br> ✓ ✓ ✓ ✓ | ✓ ✓ ✓ ✓ ✓ ✓ ✓ th-ings✓<br>                  things<br><br> ✓ ✓ ✓ ✓ <br><br> ✓ ✓ ✓ ✓ |
| A week went by. "Can the smoke stay?" asked Cam. "Please, please, please!" said the children. | ✓ ✓ ✓ ✓ ✓ ✓ ✓ <br><br> ✓ ✓ <br><br> ✓ ✓ ✓ <br><br> ✓ ✓ ✓ | ✓ ✓ came \|SC ✓ ✓ ✓ ✓<br>   went\| <br><br> ✓ ✓ <br><br> ✓ ✓ ✓ <br><br> ✓ ✓ ✓ | ✓ ✓ ✓ ✓ ✓ ✓ ✓ stand<br>                 stay<br><br> ✓ ✓ <br><br> ✓ ✓ ✓ <br><br> ✓ ✓ ✓ |
| "Yes, the smoke can stay," said Miss Blake happily. And she did not sneeze, not even once. | ✓ ✓ ✓ ✓ <br><br> ✓ ✓ ✓ ✓ <br><br> ✓ ✓ ✓ ✓ ✓ ✓ at   all<br>                    even once | ✓ ✓ ✓ ✓ <br><br> ✓ ✓ ✓ ✓ <br><br> ✓ ✓ ✓ ✓ ✓ ✓ ✓ | ✓ ✓ ✓ ✓ <br><br> ✓ ✓ ✓ hungrily<br>      happily<br><br> ✓ ✓ ✓ ✓ ✓ ✓ ✓ |

| Total # of Running Words 301 | Running Record 1 | Running Record 2 | Running Record 3 |
|---|---|---|---|
| # of Errors | | | |
| # of Self-Corrections | | | |

**Accuracy Rate**

$$\frac{RW - E}{RW} \times 100 = \%$$

**Self-Correction Rate**

$$\frac{SC}{E + SC} = SC \text{ Rate}$$

| **Guiding Questions** | **Your Thoughts** |
|---|---|

**Guiding Questions**

- What are the strengths and needs of each child?
- What do these records have in common?
- How would I use this information to plan instruction?

An answer key is provided at the end of the chapter.

How did you respond to the guiding questions? Were you able to identify each child's strengths and needs? Do you know what type of instruction each child needs next, to help him or her become a better reader? Because we only asked you to calculate the accuracy and self-correction rates, answering the questions may have been challenging. All three of the running records indicate the same accuracy and self-correction rates, but upon closer examination, you will find differences, which should influence your instructional planning, as well as your in-the-moment decision making. In the past, if you have only used rates to determine a child's text level, these records should highlight the importance of going beyond them to better understand how children may be reading at a similar level but have very different instructional needs.

# ANALYZING THE SOURCES OF INFORMATION: MSV

When analyzing the errors and self-corrections in a running record, look for the sources of information used and neglected by the child. As you will recall from Chapter 2, the sources of information are organized into three broad categories: meaning, structure, and visual information. Multiple elements comprise each source, and the child's use of those elements is influenced by his or her place on the continuum of reading development.

As a child progresses, the sources are activated in more complex ways to support his or her evolving proficiency. For example, a beginning reader who attends to the initial letter and sound of a word is successfully using visual information, which suggests that he or she is developing the expectation that what is said should match what is seen. A child who *only* attends to the initial letters and sounds in words in higher-level text is in danger of developing a theory of reading as guessing. Reading is not guessing! The use of visual information should become more sophisticated over time, and children should quickly move beyond attending to only initial letters and sounds of words. They must learn to use units of visual information efficiently, in a sequential manner, while integrating meaning and structure.

The same could be said about the evolution of children's use of meaning and structure. At emergent text levels, meaning is often tied to the picture and is created at the sentence or page level. As texts increase in difficulty and complexity, meaning is created at a more global level. Children cannot rely solely on the pictures. They have to construct meaning from the words in the text and the overarching themes. Structure also evolves, as literary language, and sentence structures in more complex texts do not match children's everyday language as they once did in beginning texts.

## Recording MSV

To begin the analysis of errors and self-corrections, record the first letters for each of the information sources in the final two-part column of the recording sheet, Information Used. For an error, write M S V in the Error column. For a self-correction, write M S V in both the Error and Self-Correction columns. The example below shows where to put "M S V" for errors and self-corrections.

| Text | Running Record | Count | | Information Used | |
|---|---|---|---|---|---|
| | | E | SC | E<br>M S V | SC<br>M S V |
| <br>A week went by. "Can the snake stay?" asked Cam.<br>"Please, please, please!" said the children. | ✓✓✓✓✓✓✓ stand / stay<br>✓✓<br>✓✓✓<br>✓✓✓ | 1 | | M S V | |
| <br>A week went by. "Can the snake stay?" asked Cam.<br>"Please, please, please!" said the children. | ✓✓ came \| SC ✓✓✓✓✓ / went \|<br>✓✓<br>✓✓✓<br>✓✓✓ | | 1 | M S V | M S V |

## Analyzing Children's Use of Meaning

Reading is more than just saying the words on the page. It involves constructing and using meaning. Indeed, young children and adults alike should expect reading to make sense! Children bring much to the act of reading, including background knowledge about particular concepts and related vocabulary. Language and literary structures assist children in understanding text and in thinking inferentially about characters, setting, problem and solution, and overarching themes such as friendship, hope, and perseverance.

Children's reading at the sentence level must make sense, but it has to make sense at the text level also. For example, while reading a story about a giant, a child reads, *The tiger roared,* when the text says, *The giant roared.* While *a tiger roared* makes sense according to the child's understanding of the world, it does not make sense within the context of this story.

Young children will often take their eyes off the print to search the illustrations or photographs when reading. When this occurs, they are searching for meaning. Images in early texts often carry information about story elements such as setting and the characters' feelings, or the concepts presented in nonfiction. It's important to be cognizant of the fact that children will sometimes use information in the images to make up or invent the text. Inventing text and other unproductive behaviors are discussed in greater detail in Part III.

### Errors Involving M

When a child makes an error, ask yourself whether the text's meaning contributed to it. In other words, check if the error makes sense at the whole-text level, not just the sentence level. If a text says *pony*, a child using meaning may substitute it with *horse* because he looked at the picture, which clearly shows a four-legged animal with a mane and long tail. The child may also say *horse*, which can be considered a pet, because he is using meaning as a feed-forward mechanism to anticipate the word. While it is important to recognize the child's use of meaning, he ignored the available visual information—the letter *p* at the beginning of *pony*—which is problematic.

For this example, you would circle M in the Information Used/Error (E) column to show that the child used meaning while reading.

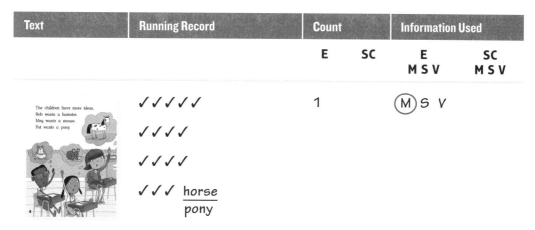

| Text | Running Record | Count | | Information Used | |
|------|---------------|-------|-----|------------------|------|
| | | **E** | **SC** | **E**<br>**M S V** | **SC**<br>**M S V** |
| | ✓ ✓ ✓ ✓ ✓<br>✓ ✓ ✓<br>✓ ✓ ✓<br>✓ ✓ ✓ $\frac{\text{horse}}{\text{pony}}$ | 1 | | Ⓜ S V | |

Now, examine Running Record 1 to see if you can find a pattern of the child using meaning but neglecting visual information, similar to $\frac{\text{horse}}{\text{pony}}$.

## Analyzing Children's Use of Structure

Just as children will use meaning to anticipate as they read, they will also use their knowledge of oral language and grammatical structures. Connecting oral language to print provides children with a rich resource. Engaging them in conversations that extend and enrich their ideas helps them understand the complexities of English and the grammar that governs it. Read-alouds expose children to literary language and text structures they will encounter when reading more difficult and complex texts.

### Errors Involving S

When an error occurs, ask yourself whether it was influenced by the child's understanding of language structure and grammar. As you analyze the record, consider the reading up to and including the error and whether the error reflects the child's oral language. Often children's oral language does not directly match what appears in text. Nonetheless, we must consider whether the way the sentence is structured prompted the child's error.

When a child makes an error on the first word in a sentence, ask yourself whether the sentence could begin that way. If the answer is "yes," then circle S for structure in the Information Used/Error column. When a child substitutes the same part of speech, such as one adjective for another, he or she is maintaining structural integrity. *Miss Blake and the Pet Snake* takes place at an elementary school. The children in the book ask about the type of pet they may get for their classroom. The question is framed, *Can we get a [adjective] [noun]?* Imagine a reader saying, *Can we get a soft cookie?* for *Can we get a soft bunny?* Structurally that sentence is correct, as *cookie* and *bunny* are both nouns, but *cookie* does not make sense in the story. If the student had said *rabbit* for *bunny*, the error would have been coded as using M for meaning (it makes sense) and S for structure (both are nouns) in the Information Used/Error column. Because meaning is embedded in language, the two are often inextricably linked. That's why, when an error like *rabbit/bunny* occurs, we circle both the M and S.

For this example, you would circle S for the error in the Information Used/Error column to show that the child attended to structure, because *cookie* and *bunny* are both nouns. However, *cookie* for *bunny* does not make sense in this story about pets. Now, take another look at Running Record 2 to see if you can find a pattern related to the child's use of structure.

| Text | Running Record | Count | | Information Used | |
|---|---|---|---|---|---|
| | | **E** | **SC** | **E**<br>**M S V** | **SC**<br>**M S V** |
| "Can we get a soft bunny?" asked Ben.<br>"Ah-choo!" said Miss Blake.<br>"Bunnies are too furry.<br>And they make me sneeze."<br>7 | ✓ ✓ ✓ ✓ ✓ cookie ✓ ✓<br>　　　　　 bunny<br><br>✓ ✓ ✓ ✓<br><br>✓ ✓ ✓ ✓<br><br>✓ ✓ ✓ ✓ ✓ | 1 | | M Ⓢ V | |

## Analyzing Children's Use of Visual Information

In simplest terms, *visual information* refers to the letters, sounds, and known words the reader processes while reading. It is the connection between the sound sequences (phonology) and the letter sequences (orthography) that represent them. It involves children's decoding attempts and the ways in which they leverage their developing knowledge. For example, beginning readers will use some letter/sound knowledge, usually the beginning letter or letter sequence, while simultaneously building a reading vocabulary of words they automatically recognize. Usually those words are meaningful to the child and include familiar names and high-frequency words that appear often in text for beginning readers. As they become more skilled, children will attend to parts of words such as the onset, rime, and ending.

Do not confuse the term *visual information* with a text's pictures and images. If a child uses a picture or image to problem-solve an unknown word, record the behavior as using meaning—not using visual information. As children progress, their use of visual information becomes more efficient, detailed, and automatic. It is also important to remember that when children are reading words correctly, they are using visual information.

## Errors Involving V

When the child makes an error, examine it and ask yourself how it visually compares to the word in the text. Do you see similarities between the two, and, if so, where do the similarities occur? Do the similarities match the letters at the beginning, middle, and/or end of the word in the text? And do you have evidence that when the child tried to solve the word, he or she used letters and sounds? Note any attention the child paid to letters and sounds on the running record. For example, the word in the text is *would*. The child first articulates the /w/, attending to the initial letter/sound. Next, the child substitutes *world* for *would*, which shows additional attention to the *-ld* at the end of the word. In the running record, those attempts should be recorded as

$$\frac{\text{w-world}}{\text{would}}$$

For this example, you would circle the V in the Information Used/Error (E) column to show that the child used visual information while reading.

| Text | Running Record | Count | | Information Used | |
|---|---|---|---|---|---|
| | | E | SC | E M S V | SC M S V |
| "We can talk about it," said Miss Blake. "What animal would make a good class pet?" | ✓ ✓ ✓ ✓ ✓ ✓ ✓  <br><br> ✓ ✓ $\frac{\text{w-world}}{\text{would}}$ ✓ ✓ ✓  <br><br> ✓ ✓ | 1 | | M S Ⓥ | |

Recording the types of visual information the child uses will assist you in identifying patterns across the child's errors. If the child's errors consistently show a visual match at the beginning and end of words, for example, it would indicate that the child is ignoring medial vowels and vowel combinations in words. Identifying and understanding error patterns has great instructional implications. Now, examine the other errors in Running Record 3 to see if you can find a pattern in the child's use of visual information, similar to *world/would*.

## Analyzing Children's Use of M S V When Self-Correcting

An error is not a random guess and does not happen by accident. There is always a reason why a child makes a substitution, insertion, or omission. For that reason, an error should be viewed as a partially correct response, because it gives the child an opportunity to use additional sources of information to self-correct. When a child self-corrects, examine the information sources he or she used and neglected in the attempt, and record them in the Information Used/Error column. Next, analyze the self-correction to determine any additional information sources the child used while problem-solving that lead to a correct response and record them in the Information Used/SC column. See examples below of various ways a reader self-corrected the errors and the information sources she used.

| Text | Running Record | Count | | Information Used | |
|---|---|---|---|---|---|
| | | E | SC | E<br>M S V | SC<br>M S V |
| 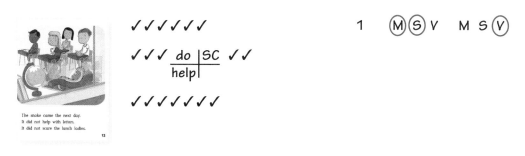 | ✓ ✓ ✓ ✓ ✓ ✓ lean \|SC ✓<br>‾‾‾‾‾‾‾‾‾‾<br>learn\|<br><br>✓ ✓ ✓<br><br>✓ ✓ sc-✓ ✓ ✓ ✓ ✓<br>‾‾‾‾‾‾<br>scare<br><br>✓ ✓<br><br>✓ ✓ ✓ ✓ ✓<br><br>✓ ✓ ✓ | | 1 | M S Ⓥ | Ⓜ Ⓢ V |

The child used visual information (initial letter, vowel combination, and final letter) when she read *lean* for *learn*. Then she used meaning and structure to self-correct.

| | ✓ ✓ ✓ ✓ ✓ ✓<br><br>✓ ✓ ✓ do \|SC ✓ ✓<br>‾‾‾‾‾‾‾‾‾<br>help\|<br><br>✓ ✓ ✓ ✓ ✓ ✓ | | 1 | Ⓜ Ⓢ V | M S Ⓥ |

The child used meaning and structure when she substituted *do* for *help*. When she realized the visual mismatch, she self-corrected.

| Text | Running Record | Count | | Information Used | |
|------|----------------|-------|------|------------------|------|
| | | E | SC | E<br>M S V | SC<br>M S V |
| | They \| SC ✓ ✓ ✓ ✓ ✓ ✓<br>Then \|<br><br>✓ ✓ ✓ ✓ ✓<br><br>✓ ✓<br><br>✓ ✓ ✓ ✓ ✓ ✓<br><br>✓ ✓ ✓ | | 1 | Ⓜ Ⓢ Ⓥ | M S Ⓥ |

The child made an integrated attempt, using all three sources of information, when she read *They* for *Then*. She may have noticed the visual mismatch at the end of the word and self-corrected.

## Analyzing Tolds

If a child makes an attempt and recognizes something is amiss, but does not continue reading, give a Told and analyze the attempt just as any other error. If the child does not make an attempt at the unknown word and verbally appeals for help, give a Told. Since the child took no action on the challenging word, you have nothing to analyze. You can still write M S V in the Information Used column, but don't circle any of the information sources.

# FROM PRACTICE TO PROFICIENCY

Analyze the complete running record below, which is a reading of *Miss Blake and the Pet Snake* by Myka-Lynne Sokoloff (running words: 301). Be sure to tally and analyze the errors and self-corrections, and calculate the accuracy and self-correction rates. An answer key is available at the end of the chapter.

| Text | Running Record | Count | | Information Used | |
|---|---|---|---|---|---|
| | | E | SC | E<br>M S V | SC<br>M S V |
| "Good morning, class," said Miss Blake.<br>"Good morning," said the class. | ✓ ✓ ✓ ✓ ✓<br>✓ ✓ ✓ ✓ ✓ | | | | |
| "Can we get a class pet?" asked Dan.<br>"I'm not sure," said Miss Blake.<br>"Please, please, please!" said the children. | ✓ ✓ ✓ ✓ $\frac{\text{clever}}{\text{class}}$ ✓ ✓ ✓<br>✓ $\frac{\text{never}}{\text{not}}$ \| SC ✓ ✓ ✓ ✓<br>✓ ✓ ✓<br>✓ ✓ ✓ | | | | |
| "We can talk about it," said Miss Blake.<br>"What animal would make a good class pet?" | ✓ ✓ ✓ $\frac{\text{A}}{\text{about}}$ \| T ✓ ✓ ✓ ✓<br>✓ ✓ $\frac{\text{will}}{\text{would}}$ ✓ ✓ ✓<br>✓ ✓ | | | | |

| Text | Running Record | Count | | Information Used | |
|------|----------------|-------|-----|------------------|-----|
| | | E | SC | E<br>M S V | SC<br>M S V |

✓ <u>raced</u> |SC ✓✓✓✓✓<br>   <u>raised</u>|

✓ ✓ ✓ ✓

✓ ✓ ✓ ✓ ✓ ✓ ✓

✓ ✓ ✓ ✓ ✓

✓ ✓ ✓ ✓ <u>think</u>   ✓ ✓<br>       <u>thought</u>

✓ ✓ ✓ ✓

✓ ✓ ✓ ✓ ✓ ✓ ✓ <u>C-am</u>✓<br>               <u>Cam</u>

✓ ✓ ✓ ✓

↓ ✓ ✓ ✓ <u>fur</u> |R |SC<br>       <u>furry</u>|

✓ ✓ ✓ ✓ ✓

✓ ✓ ✓ ✓ ✓ ✓ ✓

✓ ✓ ✓

✓ ✓ ✓

✓ ✓ ✓ ✓ ✓

✓ ✓ ✓ ✓ ✓

✓ <u>wanted</u> ✓ ✓<br>  <u>wants</u>

✓ <u>wanted</u> ✓ ✓<br>  <u>wants</u>

✓ <u>wanted</u> ✓ ✓<br>  <u>wants</u>

| Text | Running Record | Count | | Information Used | |
|---|---|---|---|---|---|
| | | E | SC | E<br>M S V | SC<br>M S V |

Miss Blake's nose got redder.
Her eyes did, too.
"Those will not do," she said sadly.
"Ah-choo! Ah-choo! Ah-choo!"

✓ ✓ ✓ ✓ red / redder

✓ ✓ ✓ ✓

These / Those ✓ ✓ ✓ ✓ ✓ sad | SC / sadly |

✓ ✓ ✓

Then Jen raised her hand. "I have a pet snake that needs a new home," she said.

"Oh?" said Miss Blake. "I'm not sure about a snake."

They | SC ✓ ✓ ✓ ✓ ✓ ✓ ✓ / Then |

✓ ✓ ✓ ✓ ✓ ✓ ✓

✓ ✓

✓ ✓ ✓ ✓ ✓ ✓ ✓

a-b-out ✓ ✓ ✓ / about

"A pet snake can help us learn our letters," said Cam.

"It can scare the lunch ladies, too!" said Dan.

"That is not nice, Dan," said Miss Blake.

✓ ✓ ✓ ✓ ✓ ✓ ✓

✓ ✓ ✓

✓ ✓ sc-✓ ✓ ✓ ✓ ✓ / scare

✓ ✓

✓ ✓ ✓ ✓ ✓

✓ ✓ ✓

"A pet snake does not have fur," said Pat.

"Okay, we will try it," says Miss Blake.

✓ ✓ ✓ ✓ ✓ ✓ ✓

✓ ✓

✓ ✓ ✓ ✓ ✓ ✓ ✓

✓ ✓ ✓ ✓ ✓
✓ ✓ ✓ ✓ ✓
✓ ✓ ✓ ✓ ✓ ✓

✓✓✓✓✓✓✓ th-ings✓ / things
✓ ✓ ✓ ✓
✓ ✓ ✓ ✓

✓ w-ee-k✓ ✓ ✓ ✓ ✓ ✓ / week
✓ ✓
✓ ✓ ✓
✓ ✓ ✓

✓ ✓ ✓ ✓ ✓
✓ ✓ ✓ happy / happily
✓ ✓ ✓ ✓ ✓ ✓ ✓

---

**# of Errors:**                    **# of Self-Corrections:**

---

**Accuracy Rate:**

$$\frac{RW^* - E}{RW^*} \times 100 = \%$$

---

**Self-Correction Rate:**

$$\frac{SC}{E + SC} = SC\ Rate$$

---

*301

An answer key is provided at the end of the chapter.

# CLOSING THOUGHT

At first, taking, scoring, and analyzing running records may seem overwhelming. But we promise, the more you practice, the easier it gets. In time, you will wonder how you ever taught reading without them. Running records celebrate the individuality of each child's processing and the importance of differentiating our instruction.

Now that you have learned how to take, score, and analyze running records, we need to explain one more aspect of the child's processing system—one more mouse to reveal the unknown thing and complete the picture! In the next chapter, we will examine the relationship between comprehension and fluency, and how it is captured on a running record.

## Answer key to the practice activity on pages 69–73

| | Running Record 1 | Running Record 2 | Running Record 3 |
|---|---|---|---|
| **# of Errors** | 10 | 10 | 10 |
| **# of Self-Corrections** | 5 | 5 | 5 |
| **Accuracy Rate** $\dfrac{RW - E}{RW} \times 100 = \%$ | 97% | 97% | 97% |
| **Self-Correction Rate** $\dfrac{SC}{E + SC} = SC\ Rate$ | 1:3 | 1:3 | 1:3 |

At the beginning of the chapter, we posed three guiding questions, which may have been difficult to answer because the errors and self-corrections for each child had not yet been analyzed. We did this to highlight how your instructional decision making is limited if you only consider accuracy and self-correction rates. In the next two rows, we analyze the errors and self-corrections for the three running records to show how what we learn allows us to answer the guiding questions more precisely.

| | Running Record 1 | | Running Record 2 | | Running Record 3 | |
|---|---|---|---|---|---|---|
| **Analysis of Errors** | kids / class | Ⓜ Ⓢ V | do / get | Ⓜ Ⓢ V | clash / class | M S Ⓥ |
| | animal / pet | Ⓜ Ⓢ V | be / make | Ⓜ Ⓢ V | never / not | Ⓜ Ⓢ Ⓥ |
| | might / would | Ⓜ Ⓢ V | legs / hand | M Ⓢ V | world / would | M S Ⓥ |
| | hairy / furry | Ⓜ Ⓢ V | to / fact | M Ⓢ V | raced / raised | M Ⓢ Ⓥ |
| | have / get | Ⓜ Ⓢ V | laugh / sneeze | M Ⓢ V | think / thought | M S Ⓥ |
| | rabbit / bunny | Ⓜ Ⓢ V | cookie / bunny | M Ⓢ V | hamstore / hamster | M S Ⓥ |
| | horse / pony | Ⓜ Ⓢ V | henhouse / hamster | M Ⓢ Ⓥ | muse / mouse | M S Ⓥ |
| | skin / fur | Ⓜ Ⓢ V | prize / mouse | M Ⓢ V | these / those | Ⓜ Ⓢ Ⓥ |
| | at / even | Ⓜ Ⓢ V | ice cream / pony | M Ⓢ V | stand / stay | M Ⓢ Ⓥ |
| | all / once | Ⓜ Ⓢ V | time / day | Ⓜ Ⓢ V | hungrily / happily | M Ⓢ Ⓥ |
| **Analysis of Self-Corrections** | messy / furry | Ⓜ Ⓢ V  M S Ⓥ | snack / snake | M Ⓢ Ⓥ  Ⓜ S V | fur / furry | M S Ⓥ  Ⓜ Ⓢ V |
| | face / nose | Ⓜ Ⓢ V  M S Ⓥ | school / letters | M Ⓢ V  Ⓜ Ⓢ Ⓥ | reader / redder | M S Ⓥ  Ⓜ Ⓢ V |
| | they / then | Ⓜ Ⓢ Ⓥ  M S Ⓥ | big / nice | Ⓜ Ⓢ V  M S Ⓥ | satly / sadly | M S Ⓥ  Ⓜ Ⓢ V |
| | teach / learn | Ⓜ Ⓢ V  M S Ⓥ | and / but | Ⓜ Ⓢ V  M S Ⓥ | they / then | Ⓜ Ⓢ Ⓥ  M S V |
| | do / help | Ⓜ Ⓢ V  M S Ⓥ | came / went | Ⓜ Ⓢ V  M S Ⓥ | lean / learn | M S Ⓥ  Ⓜ Ⓢ V |

| Guiding Questions | Running Record 1 | Running Record 2 | Running Record 3 |
|---|---|---|---|
| **What are the strengths of each child?** | From the analysis of errors and self-corrections, it is evident that the child reads for meaning and maintains structural integrity, but at times neglects the visual information. | From the analysis of errors and self-corrections, it is evident that the child is relying on oral language, and while his attempts maintain structural integrity, they usually do not make sense and lack attention to visual information. | From the analysis of errors and self-corrections, it is evident that the child always uses initial visual information and often attends to the visual information at the end of the word. There are times when the child shows evidence of attending to medial vowel sounds. |
| **How would you use this information to plan instruction?** | Instruction in decoding is needed. At this text level, the child should at the very least be attending to initial letter and sound information. | Instruction in decoding is needed. Further, the child needs to attend to the meaning of the story. | Instruction needs to be focused on attending to meaning and searching sequentially across the word with particular attention to medial vowels. High-frequency words (especially ones that begin with *th-* and *w-*) need to be taught and practiced. |
| **What do these records have in common?** | All three children read the text with the same accuracy and self-correction rates. While the readings were considered successful when looking at the rates, the analysis of the errors and self-corrections provides information that will guide instructional decisions. Further, it is easy to see that while the children all read the text with 97% accuracy and 1:3 self-correction rate, their needs as readers are drastically different. | | |

## Answer key to the practice activity on pages 83–86

| Text | Running Record | Count | | Information Used | |
|---|---|---|---|---|---|
| | | **E** | **SC** | **E** **M S V** | **SC** **M S V** |
| | ✓ ✓ ✓ ✓ ✓ ✓<br>✓ ✓ ✓ ✓ | | | | |
| | ✓ ✓ ✓ ✓ clever ✓ ✓ ✓<br> ̲ ̲ ̲ ̲ ̲ ̲ ̲<br>        class<br>✓ never │SC ✓ ✓ ✓ ✓<br>   ̲ ̲ ̲ ̲ ̲ ̲ │<br>   not   │<br>✓ ✓ ✓<br>✓ ✓ ✓ | 1<br><br><br>1 | | Ⓜ Ⓢ Ⓥ<br><br>Ⓜ Ⓢ Ⓥ | <br><br>M S Ⓥ |
| | ✓ ✓ ✓  A   │ ✓ ✓ ✓ ✓<br>      ̲ ̲ ̲ ̲ ̲ │<br>     about│T<br>✓ ✓  will   ✓ ✓ ✓<br>    ̲ ̲ ̲ ̲ ̲<br>    would<br>✓ ✓ | 1<br><br><br>1 | | M S V<br><br>Ⓜ Ⓢ Ⓥ | |
| | ✓ raced │SC ✓✓✓✓✓✓<br>  ̲ ̲ ̲ ̲ ̲ ̲ │<br>  raised│<br>✓ ✓ ✓<br>✓ ✓ ✓ ✓ ✓ ✓ ✓<br>✓ ✓ ✓ ✓ ✓<br>✓ ✓ ✓ think  ✓ ✓<br>      ̲ ̲ ̲ ̲ ̲ ̲<br>      thought<br>✓ ✓ ✓ ✓ | 1<br><br><br><br><br><br>1 | | M Ⓢ Ⓥ<br><br><br><br><br><br>Ⓜ S Ⓥ | Ⓜ S V |

| Text | Running Record | Count | | Information Used | |
|------|----------------|-------|-----|-----------------|-----|
| | | E | SC | E<br>M S V | SC<br>M S V |
| | ✓ ✓ ✓ ✓ ✓ ✓ ✓ $\frac{\text{C-am✓}}{\text{Cam}}$ | | | | |
| | ✓ ✓ ✓ | | | | |
| | ↓✓ ✓ ✓ $\frac{\text{fur}}{\text{furry}}$ \| R \| SC | 1 | | M S Ⓥ | Ⓜ Ⓢ Ⓥ |
| | ✓ ✓ ✓ ✓ ✓ | | | | |
| | ✓ ✓ ✓ ✓ ✓ ✓ ✓ ✓ | | | | |
| | ✓ ✓ ✓ ✓ | | | | |
| | ✓ ✓ ✓ ✓ | | | | |
| | ✓ ✓ ✓ ✓ ✓ | | | | |
| | ✓ ✓ ✓ ✓ ✓ | | | | |
| | ✓ $\frac{\text{wanted}}{\text{wants}}$ ✓ ✓ | 1 | | Ⓜ Ⓢ Ⓥ | |
| | ✓ $\frac{\text{wanted}}{\text{wants}}$ ✓ ✓ | 1 | | Ⓜ Ⓢ Ⓥ | |
| | ✓ $\frac{\text{wanted}}{\text{wants}}$ ✓ ✓ | 1 | | Ⓜ Ⓢ Ⓥ | |
| | ✓ ✓ ✓ ✓ $\frac{\text{red}}{\text{redder}}$ | 1 | | Ⓜ Ⓢ Ⓥ | |
| | ✓ ✓ ✓ ✓ | | | Ⓜ Ⓢ Ⓥ | |
| | $\frac{\text{These}}{\text{Those}}$ ✓✓✓✓✓ $\frac{\text{sad}}{\text{sadly}}$ \| SC | 1 | 1 | Ⓜ S Ⓥ | M Ⓢ Ⓥ |
| | ✓ ✓ ✓ | | | | |

| Text | Running Record | Count | | Information Used | |
|------|----------------|-------|---|------------------|---|
| | | E | SC | E<br>M S V | SC<br>M S V |

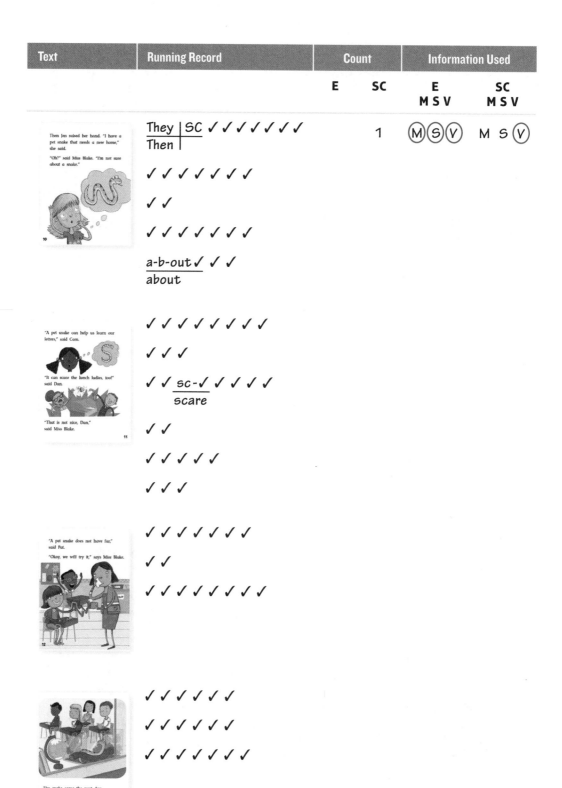

Running Record section:

Then Jen raised her hand. "I have a pet snake that needs a new home," she said.

"Oh?" said Miss Blake. "I'm not sure about a snake."

They | SC ✓ ✓ ✓ ✓ ✓ ✓  — Count SC: 1 — Information Used E: Ⓜ Ⓢ Ⓥ — SC: M S Ⓥ
Then |

✓ ✓ ✓ ✓ ✓ ✓

✓ ✓

✓ ✓ ✓ ✓ ✓ ✓

a-b-out ✓ ✓ ✓
about

---

"A pet snake can help us learn our letters," said Cam.

"It can scare the lunch ladies, too!" said Dan.

"That is not nice, Dan," said Miss Blake.

✓ ✓ ✓ ✓ ✓ ✓ ✓

✓ ✓ ✓

✓ ✓  sc-✓ ✓ ✓ ✓
    scare

✓ ✓

✓ ✓ ✓ ✓

✓ ✓ ✓

---

"A pet snake does not have fur," said Pat.

"Okay, we will try it," says Miss Blake.

✓ ✓ ✓ ✓ ✓ ✓

✓ ✓

✓ ✓ ✓ ✓ ✓ ✓ ✓

---

The snake came the next day.
It did not help with letters.
It did not scare the lunch ladies.

✓ ✓ ✓ ✓ ✓

✓ ✓ ✓ ✓ ✓

✓ ✓ ✓ ✓ ✓ ✓

| Text | Running Record | Count | | Information Used | |
|---|---|---|---|---|---|
| | | **E** | **SC** | **E**<br>**M S V** | **SC**<br>**M S V** |
|  | ✓ ✓ ✓ ✓ ✓ ✓ ✓ th-ings✓<br>‎ things<br><br>✓ ✓ ✓ ✓<br><br>✓ ✓ ✓ | | | | |
|  | ✓ w-ee-k✓ ✓ ✓ ✓ ✓ ✓<br>‎ week<br><br>✓ ✓<br><br>✓ ✓ ✓<br><br>✓ ✓ ✓ | | | | |
| | ✓ ✓ ✓ ✓ ✓<br><br>✓ ✓ ✓ happy<br>‎ happily<br><br>✓ ✓ ✓ ✓ ✓ ✓ ✓ ✓ | 1 | | Ⓜ S Ⓥ | |

---

**# of Errors:**  10          **# of Self-Corrections:**  5

---

**Accuracy Rate: 97%**

$$\frac{301 - E}{301} \times 100 = \%$$          $$\frac{301 - 10}{301} = \frac{291}{301} = .966 \times 100 = 97\%$$

---

**Self-Correction Rate: 1:3**

$$\frac{SC}{E + SC} = SC\ Rate$$          $$\frac{5}{10 + 5} = \frac{5}{15} = \frac{1}{3} = 1:3$$

---

# CHAPTER 6

# Checking Fluency and Comprehension

**W**hile taking a running record, you have an ideal opportunity to assess fluency and comprehension. You can listen for how the child groups words and uses pauses, pitch, and/or tone. You can also note how the reading sounds. You can check the emphasis the child places on certain words, which is an indicator of understanding, and the pace or rate at which the child reads. Fluency and comprehension are inextricably linked. The way a child's reading sounds offers insight into his or her construction of meaning. Assessing for fluency and comprehension has great implications for instructional decision making.

But before we explore fluency and comprehension, let's revisit the running record from the previous chapter, which appears on the following pages. The child's accuracy rate of 97 percent and self-correction rate of 1:3 indicate that she read the text well. Review the sources of information the child used and neglected. Taking those sources into account, what do you think of her reading? What additional information would assist you in answering that question?

| Text | Running Record | Count | | Information Used | |
|---|---|---|---|---|---|
| | | E | SC | E<br>M S V | SC<br>M S V |
| "Good morning, class," said Miss Blake.<br>"Good morning," said the class. | ✓ ✓ ✓ ✓ ✓ ✓<br>✓ ✓ ✓ ✓ ✓ | | | | |
| "Can we get a class pet?" asked Dan.<br>"I'm not sure," said Miss Blake.<br>"Please, please, please!" said the children. | ✓ ✓ ✓ ✓ clash/class ✓ ✓ ✓<br>✓ never/not ✓ ✓ ✓ ✓<br>✓ ✓ ✓<br>✓ ✓ ✓ | 1<br>1 | | M S Ⓥ<br>Ⓜ Ⓢ Ⓥ | |
| "We can talk about it," said Miss Blake.<br>"What animal would make a good class pet?" | ✓ ✓ ✓ ✓ ✓ ✓ ✓ ✓<br>✓ ✓ world/would ✓ ✓ ✓<br>✓ ✓ | 1 | | M S Ⓥ | |
| Dan raised his hand. "Can we get a little dog?" asked Dan.<br>"Dogs are too furry and they make me sneeze," said Miss Blake.<br>"In fact, just the thought of them makes me sneeze. Ah-choo!" | ✓ raced/raised ✓ ✓ ✓ ✓ ✓<br>✓ ✓ ✓ ✓<br>✓ ✓ ✓ ✓ ✓ ✓<br>✓ ✓ ✓ ✓ ✓<br>✓ ✓ ✓ ✓ think/thought ✓ ✓<br>✓ ✓ ✓ ✓ | 1<br>1 | | M Ⓢ Ⓥ<br>M S Ⓥ | |

| Text | Running Record | Count | | Information Used | |
|------|---------------|-------|-----|-----------------|------|
| | | **E** | **SC** | **E**<br>**M S V** | **SC**<br>**M S V** |

✓ ✓ ✓ ✓ ✓ ✓ ✓ C-am ✓

✓ ✓ ✓

↓
✓ ✓ ✓  fur | R | SC
       furry |

✓ ✓ ✓ ✓ ✓               **1**      M S Ⓥ   Ⓜ Ⓢ V

✓ ✓ ✓ ✓ ✓ ✓ ✓

✓ ✓ ✓

✓ ✓ ✓

✓ ✓ ✓ ✓ ✓

✓ ✓ ✓ ✓

✓ ✓ ✓  ham store      **1**        M S Ⓥ
       hamster

✓ ✓ ✓  muse          **1**        M S Ⓥ
       mouse

✓ ✓ ✓ ✓

✓ ✓ ✓ ✓  reader | SC      **1**     M S Ⓥ   Ⓜ Ⓢ V
          redder |

✓ ✓ ✓ ✓

These ✓ ✓ ✓ ✓ ✓ satly | SC   **1**   **1**   Ⓜ Ⓢ Ⓥ
Those           sadly |
                                M S Ⓥ   Ⓜ Ⓢ V

✓ ✓ ✓

| Text | Running Record | Count | | Information Used | |
|---|---|---|---|---|---|
| | | E | SC | E M S V | SC M S V |
| Then Jen raised her hand. "I have a pet snake that needs a new home," she said. "Oh?" said Miss Blake. "I'm not sure about a snake." | They \| SC ✓ ✓ ✓ ✓ ✓ ✓<br>Then \|<br><br>✓ ✓ ✓ ✓ ✓ ✓<br><br>✓ ✓<br><br>✓ ✓ ✓ ✓ ✓ ✓ ✓<br><br>a-b-out ✓ ✓ ✓<br>about | 1 | | Ⓜ Ⓢ Ⓥ | M S Ⓥ |
| "A pet snake can help us learn our letters," said Cam. "It can scare the lunch ladies, too!" said Dan. "That is not nice, Dan," said Miss Blake. | ✓ ✓ ✓ ✓ ✓ ✓ lean \| SC ✓<br>learn \|<br><br>✓ ✓ ✓<br><br>✓ ✓ SC✓ ✓ ✓ ✓ ✓<br><br>✓ ✓<br><br>✓ ✓ ✓ ✓ ✓<br><br>✓ ✓ ✓ | 1 | | M S Ⓥ | Ⓜ Ⓢ V |
| "A pet snake does not have fur," said Pat. "Okay, we will try it," says Miss Blake. | ✓ ✓ ✓ ✓ ✓ ✓<br><br>✓ ✓<br><br>✓ ✓ ✓ ✓ ✓ ✓ ✓ | | | | |
| The snake came the next day. It did not help with letters. It did not scare the lunch ladies. | ✓ ✓ ✓ ✓ ✓<br><br>✓ ✓ ✓ ✓ ✓<br><br>✓ ✓ ✓ ✓ ✓ ✓ | | | | |

| Text | Running Record | Count | | Information Used | |
|------|----------------|-------|------|-----------------|------|
| | | E | SC | E M S V | SC M S V |
| But the snake did do a few fun things. It sat on laps. It gave nice hugs. | ✓ ✓ ✓ ✓ ✓ ✓ ✓ th-ings✓ / things  ✓ ✓ ✓ ✓  ✓ ✓ ✓ ✓ | | | | |
| A week went by. "Can the snake stay?" asked Cam. "Please, please, please!" said the children. | ✓ ✓ ✓ ✓ ✓ ✓ ✓ stand / stay  ✓ ✓  ✓ ✓ ✓  ✓ ✓ ✓ | 1 | | M Ⓢ Ⓥ | |
| "Yes, the snake can stay," said Miss Blake happily. And she did not sneeze, not even once. | ✓ ✓ ✓ ✓ ✓  ✓ ✓ ✓ hungrily / happily  ✓ ✓ ✓ ✓ ✓ ✓ ✓ ✓ | 1 | | M Ⓢ Ⓥ | |

## ASSESSING FLUENCY

Without any information about how the child read the book—what her reading sounded like, in other words—we can't be sure if her reading was as good as the numbers indicate. You may take the time to assess reading fluency and its many dimensions, but if you don't record the information on the running record, it will be lost. Ask yourself: After listening to 20 different children read during the day, will I remember how one child's reading of *Miss Blake and the Pet Snake* sounded? Probably not. The record is one-dimensional, without a statement about the child's fluency. By recording a statement about fluency, along with the accuracy and self-correction rates and the analysis of errors and self-corrections, you will have a more complete picture of the reader.

Now, consider the following statement about the child's reading of *Miss Blake and the Pet Snake*, keeping in mind that the way a child reads words in phrases gives insight into his or her comprehension of the text.

"The child's reading was choppy, slow, and labored. She read word by word and ignored the punctuation."

How does this change your thinking about the child's reading of the book? Look back at her errors and the sources of information she used. Notice that meaning was often neglected. Furthermore, the reading was choppy, slow, and labored. When children do not use meaning as a feed-forward mechanism, that's the way they typically read. Recording a statement about fluency provides another data point to better understand the child's processing.

## Elements of Fluency

To help you understand the elements of fluency, we provide the chart below, which lists each element, defines it, and suggests ways to record it on the running record.

| Element | Definition | How to Record It |
|---|---|---|
| **Phrasing** | The grouping of words into meaningful units. | ✓ ✓ ✓　　in the woods<br><br>The line drawn under the three checks indicates the child read the prepositional phrase as a meaningful unit. This is mainly recorded when a child is having difficulty with phrasing and you see evidence that he is grouping words. Recording this information will help you identify patterns of phrasing. For example, where is the child grouping words? Does the phrasing occur on speaker tags, prepositional phrases, or introductory clauses? You may make note of the specifics, or you may record the number of words in the grouping, such as, *"The child read 3–4 word phrases."* |
| **Punctuation** | The appropriate pausing or stopping at the various punctuation marks. | ✓ ✓ ✓⊙✓ ✓ ✓<br><br>It is important to mark the record showing where the child ignored the punctuation. In this example, the reader ignored the period and read on. This can greatly affect meaning and limit the child's ability to self-correct. If the reader is regularly attending to punctuation, there is no reason to record anything. |
| **Expression/ Intonation** | The rise and fall of voice, to indicate a question or change in tone, or stress of certain words or words in bold to convey meaning. | The use of or lack of expression and intonation can be noted in a statement at the end of the record.<br><br>"The child's reading was flat. His pitch and tone did not change on the words in bold."<br><br>"The reading sounded robotic and lacked expression."<br><br>"The child read with expression." |

| Element | Definition | How to Record It |
|---|---|---|
| Rate | The pace or speed of the reading, which is often calculated in words per minute. | When the reading is phrased and fluent, which is a reflection that meaning is being used as a source of information, the words read per minute will be in the acceptable range. If you are required to report a child's reading rate, you can time the running record and calculate the words read per minute at the end. If the reading is word-by-word, it is important to note this to see if a pattern emerges over time that would indicate a problem. |

## Fluency Rubrics

In addition to writing a statement about the child's fluency, you may choose to use a rubric or scale (NAEP, 2002), such as the one below, to rate the child's reading from 0–3. The descriptions in it may also serve as starting points in crafting your own statement about a child's reading that is more nuanced and better captures how he or she sounded while reading.

**Fluency Rubric**

| Rating | Description |
|---|---|
| 0 | Slow or choppy word-by-word reading with no expression. |
| 1 | Moderately slow reading with 2 or 3 words grouped together. Little expression. |
| 2 | Acceptable reading rate with 3 to 4 words grouped in meaningful phrases most of the time. Some expression. |
| 3 | Phrased and fluent reading with appropriate intonation and expression. |

# ASSESSING COMPREHENSION

After the reading, discuss the text with the child before attending to any teaching points. This sends the message to the child that gaining meaning from text is what reading is all about. There are several ways to assess the child's comprehension, as outlined in the chart below.

| Assessment | Description | Example From *Miss Blake and the Pet Snake* |
|---|---|---|
| **Conversations After the Reading** | After the reading, ask the child about the characters or events in the text. Some of the questions should ask the child to combine the information in the text with his own ideas. Remember this should be a conversation, not an interrogation. Ask open-ended questions and invite the child to make connections with the story and her own experiences. With nonfiction texts, engage the child in a conversation about the content and important information and key facts that give insight into the child's understanding of the topic. | Some examples of conversation starters:<br><br>• "How did you feel about this story?"<br><br>• "Why do you think the snake was a good pet for Miss Blake?"<br><br>• "Do you have a pet at home and if not, what kind of pet would you like? Why is this a good pet for you?" |

| Assessment | Description | Example From *Miss Blake and the Pet Snake* |
|---|---|---|
| **Retellings** | After the reading, the child is invited to retell the events of the story. The teacher should note whether the events were in proper sequence and whether the child was able to infer the main ideas. With nonfiction text, the child should retell the main ideas and key facts related to the content. The teacher should note if only basic information is given or if the child is able to provide details. A rubric can be used to score the retelling. | Ask the student to retell the story. Say, "Tell me what happened in this book." You may prompt the student by saying, "Tell me more" or "What else happened?" When using a rubric to rate the retelling, prompting the child for more information does not lower the score.<br><br>**Retelling Rubric**<br><br>**0** Recalls no important facts/events.<br><br>**1** Recalls a limited number of important facts/events.<br><br>**2** Recalls some important facts/events.<br><br>**3** Recalls most of the important facts/events. |
| **Formalized Comprehension Checks** | When taking running records as part of a benchmark assessment, you will usually administer a formalized comprehension check, such as the one used in this table from the *Next Steps in Guided Reading Assessment*. The comprehension check typically involves a series of questions that ask children to identify key details, evaluate and infer elements of the text, analyze characters, and contextually define vocabulary. The comprehension check is scored against the provided answers. | **Key Detail:** "What different kinds of animals do the students suggest as class pets?"<br><br>**Evaluation:** "Do you think a pony is a good class pet? Why or why not?"<br><br>**Inference:** "Why do you think the furry animals make Miss Blake sneeze?"<br><br>**Character Analysis:** "What is a word that describes Dan?"<br><br>**Vocabulary:** "Can you think of another animal that would make a good class pet for Miss Blake?" |

After the fluency statement in the running record for *Miss Blake and the Pet Snake*, the teacher added, *The child could answer few questions about the story and was unable to think inferentially.* This statement provides further evidence that the child may not be using and constructing meaning while reading and, as a result, is having some difficulty comprehending text. Despite her high accuracy rate and acceptable self-correction rate, other factors, such as her word-by-word reading and over-reliance on visual information producing errors that do not make sense, suggest her need for targeted instruction in constructing meaning.

All information in the running record (e.g., accuracy rate, self-correction rate, information sources used, fluency statement, and comprehension statement) should influence the teacher's selection of texts for instruction and how she introduces them. The information should also inform the ways she prompts and questions the child while reading. This will be discussed in greater detail in Part III.

## Comprehension Rubrics

In addition to the assessments described earlier, you may choose to use a rubric, such as the ones below, to rate the child's reading from 0–3.

### Literal Comprehension Rubric

| Rating | Description |
| --- | --- |
| 0 | Recalls no important facts/events. |
| 1 | Recalls a limited number of important facts/events. |
| 2 | Recalls some important facts/events. |
| 3 | Recalls most of the important facts/events. |

### Deeper Comprehension Rubric

| Rating | Description |
| --- | --- |
| 0 | Shows no understanding of inferences or deeper meaning. |
| 1 | Shows limited understanding of inferences or deeper meaning. |
| 2 | Shows some understanding of inferences or deeper meaning. |
| 3 | Shows full understanding of inferences or deeper meaning. |

## CLOSING THOUGHT

As Part II draws to a close, we hope that you have a better understanding of how to take, score, and analyze a running record. When we capture all possible information about a child's reading, we have a more complete picture of its complexities. If we examine only one part, as each of the mice did in Ed Young's *Seven Blind Mice*, we may describe the child's processing inaccurately and, as a result, make misinformed instructional decisions.

# Making Informed Instructional Decisions Using Running Records

The chapters in Part III focus on instructional decision-making, inspired by your analysis of running records. Based on our many years of experience, we discuss four major, but often overlooked, issues that occur when analyzing running records: student monitoring, appeals for help, recognition of high-frequency words, and use of visual information, all of which require targeted attention. Each chapter provides an overview of the issue, how to recognize it through analysis, and how to address it in instruction.

**VIDEO LINK**

Visit **scholastic.com/ResourcesNSFRR** for professional videos of the authors taking, scoring, and analyzing running records.

# CHAPTER 7

# Detecting Ways Children Monitor

**W**hen taking a running record, it is important to capture children's verbal comments and nonverbal behaviors, in addition to their errors and self-corrections. Recording children's comments, such as "I don't know that word" or "Is that right?", provides additional clues about their problem solving. Without these anecdotal notes, we are left with a static view of a dynamic process.

The chart on the following pages captures a child's reading of *The Bears Make Fruit Salad* by Milo Kennedy (Level D; running words: 88). Pay particular attention to the teacher's anecdotal notes, which you'll find in the third column. Typically, you would record notes in the margin of the running record. You'll notice the child broke *Mother Bear puts in some red apples* into two sentences: *Mom bear cuts. In some apples.* The teacher added and circled a period to indicate how the child read the sentence. As you look more closely at the record, think about how the comments and behaviors add to your understanding of the child as a reader.

| Text | Running Record | Anecdotal Notes |
|---|---|---|
| This is the bear family. They are making fruit salad. 2 | ✓ ✓ ✓ ✓ ✓ <br><br> ✓ ✓ ✓ $\frac{a}{-}$ ✓ ✓ | Child shakes his head and says, "There's no *a*!" |
| Mother bear puts in some red apples. "Apples are the best!" she said. 3 | $\frac{Mom}{Mother}$ ✓ $\frac{cuts⊙}{puts}$ ✓ ✓ ✓ <br><br> ✓ ✓ $\frac{my}{the}$ \|SC ✓ ✓ | Child reads "Mom bear cuts." as a complete sentence. The rest of the page is read word by word. Child's face registers dissatisfaction. |
| Father bear puts in some yellow bananas. "Bananas are the best!" he said. 4 | ✓ ✓ $\frac{cuts}{puts}$ \|SC $\frac{up}{in}$ \|SC\| R ✓ <br><br> ✓ ✓ <br><br> ✓ ✓ $\frac{my}{the}$ \|SC ✓ ✓ ✓ | |
| Sister bear puts in some little grapes. "Grapes are the best!" she said. 5 | ✓ ✓ $\frac{p-✓}{puts}$ ✓ ✓ $\frac{green}{little}$ ✓ <br><br> ✓ ✓ ✓ ✓ ✓ | |
| Brother bear puts in some big oranges. "Oranges are the best!" he said. 6 | ✓ ✓ ✓ ✓ ✓ $\frac{orange}{big}$ \|SC ✓R <br><br> ✓ ✓ ✓ ✓ ✓ | |

| Text | Running Record | Anecdotal Notes |
|---|---|---|

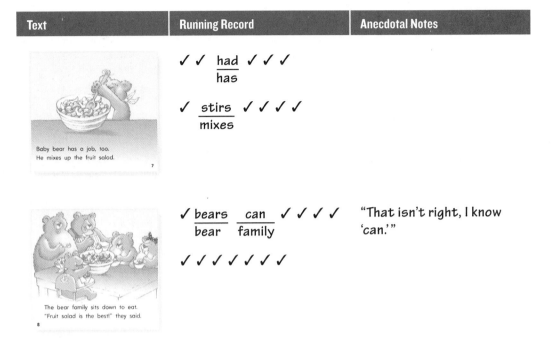

| | | |
|---|---|---|
| | ✓ ✓ had ✓ ✓ ✓<br>     ─── has | |
| | ✓ stirs ✓ ✓ ✓ ✓<br>   ─── mixes | |
| | ✓ bears can ✓ ✓ ✓ ✓<br>   ── bear ──── family<br><br>✓ ✓ ✓ ✓ ✓ ✓ | "That isn't right, I know 'can.'" |

The child's comments and some of his actions show he knows something is wrong. For example, as he read page 2, he shook his head and said, "There's no *a*!", suggesting that he recognized he had inserted a word that did not appear in the text. Other errors, such as substituting *had* for *has* and *stirs* for *mixes* on page 7, show that if an error makes sense, he ignores it and continues reading. In fact, all his errors make sense; he self-corrects only on high-frequency words that he knows, such as when he reads *my* for *the* on pages 3 and 4. On page 3, the child divides one sentence into two and tries to make the substitution meaningful. He then goes on to read *in some apples* as a unit, but quickly reverts to a word-by-word reading because he can't meaningfully connect that phrase to the second sentence on the page: *"Apples are the best!" she said*. The child's disgruntled expression indicates that he recognizes something is wrong, but he does not take action to self-correct. Recognizing something is wrong is an important reading behavior referred to as monitoring.

# WHAT IS MONITORING, AND WHY IS IT IMPORTANT?

Monitoring is being aware of when something is right and when something is wrong. A child is monitoring when he or she is reading accurately. A child is also monitoring when he or she stops in the middle of a reading, comments about an inconsistency, or even rereads. Monitoring can be viewed as checking on oneself to verify a decision. It is described in *The Literacy Dictionary: The Vocabulary of Reading and Writing* as a "conscious or metacognitive awareness" (2005, p. 229). You know a child is monitoring when something triggers him or her to search for more information. To make decisions about the words in the text, the child must confirm whether those words are meaningful, as well as structurally and visually correct. The half-right and half-wrong attempts of the child help us take instructional next steps (Clay, 2011). The half-right attempts show us what the child can control and the half-wrong attempts show us what we need to teach.

Let's explore running records for two children's readings of pages 3 to 5 in *The Bears Make Fruit Salad*. To begin, examine the sources of information Child 1 used to monitor and the implications for instruction.

## Child 1

| Text | Running Record | Count | | Information Used | |
|------|----------------|-------|------|------------------|------|
| | | E | SC | E<br>M S V | SC<br>M S V |
| Mother bear puts in some red apples.<br>"Apples are the best!" she said.<br>3 | Mom ✓ cuts⊙ ✓ ✓ ✓<br>Mother · · · puts | 2 | | (M)(S)(V)<br>(M)(S)(V) | |
| | ✓ ✓ my \|SC ✓ ✓ ✓<br>· · · the\| | | 1 | (M)(S) V | M S (V) |

### How the Child Monitored

**Mom** monitors using meaning
**Mother** and some initial visual information.

**cuts** monitors using meaning and
**puts** some ending visual information.

**my** self-corrects because he monitors
**the** on the known word *the*.

### Instructional Implication

**Mom** **cuts** Both errors show that the child
**Mother** **puts** needs to use additional visual
information while maintaining meaning
and structure.

**my** The child needs to continue to use
**the** meaning as a feed-forward system while
attending to visual information on the first
attempt.

| Text | Running Record | Count | | Information Used | |
|------|----------------|-------|---|------------------|---|
| | | **E** | **SC** | **E**<br>**M S V** | **SC**<br>**M S V** |
| Father bear puts in some yellow bananas. "Bananas are the best!" he said. 4 | ✓ ✓ cuts \|SC up \|SC\| R ✓<br>    puts\|    in \|<br>✓ ✓ | 2 | | Ⓜ Ⓢ Ⓥ<br>Ⓜ Ⓢ V | M S Ⓥ<br>M S Ⓥ |
| | ✓ ✓ my \|SC ✓ ✓ ✓<br>    the\| | 1 | | Ⓜ Ⓢ V | M S Ⓥ |

## How the Child Monitored

To fully understand this example, we begin with the substitution of *up* for *in* and the SC, because this triggers the child to reread and self-correct *cuts* for *puts*.

**up** monitors on known high-frequency
**in** word and self-corrects. The original attempt at the phrase *cuts up* for *puts in* makes sense and fits structurally, but after he self-corrects, he rereads to monitor because something was amiss.

**cuts** self-corrects *puts* when he rereads
**puts** because he notices the initial visual information.

**my** self-corrects because he monitors
**the** on known words.

## Instructional Implication

Often, errors and SCs are part of a series of actions taken by the child. To determine instructional next steps, the entire action series has to be considered. This example shows that the child is not paying close enough attention to the visual information, including known high-frequency words. Even though the child self-corrects the known words, the child is neglecting the visual information on the initial attempt. The child needs to learn to use the visual information simultaneously with meaning and structure. The child's work in this action series should be valued, but we also know that a repeated self-correction of known words produces a cognitive load that, once removed, frees the child's attention for other strategic reading work.

| Text | Running Record | Count | | Information Used | |
|---|---|---|---|---|---|
| | | E | SC | E M S V | SC M S V |
|  Sister bear puts in some little grapes. "Grapes are the best!" she said.  5 | ✓ ✓ p-✓ ✓ ✓ green ✓<br>  ⎯⎯puts⎯  ⎯⎯little⎯<br>✓ ✓ ✓ ✓ ✓ | 1 | | Ⓜ Ⓢ V | |

## How the Child Monitored

**green**
**little** — monitors using meaning but ignores the visual information.

## Instructional Implication

This example demonstrates a pattern in which the child monitors for meaning but uses little or no visual information. Monitoring for meaning is a critical first step for beginning readers. The instructional next step is to teach the student to use both meaning and visual information at the same time. At this point, the child should also be using initial letters, blends, known word parts, and high-frequency words to monitor. In this example, the child reads *green* for *little*, which makes sense and fits the pattern of the text (because, on previous pages, colors are used to describe the fruit). *Green* for *little*, however, is a gross visual error and should be addressed as part of instruction. The use of visual information changes over time and becomes more sophisticated and detailed.

Next, examine how Child 2 read the same pages, paying particularly close attention to the sources of information she used to monitor while reading. The instructional implications for Child 1 and Child 2 are very different.

## Child 2

| Text | Running Record | Count | | Information Used | |
|------|----------------|-------|-----|------------------|------|
| | | **E** | **SC** | **E**<br>**M S V** | **SC**<br>**M S V** |

| Text | Running Record | E | SC | E (M S V) | SC (M S V) |
|------|----------------|---|-----|-----------|-----|
| Mother bear puts in some red apples. "Apples are the best!" she said. 3 | ✓ ✓ <u>plays</u> ✓ ✓ ✓ ✓<br>    puts | 1 | | M ⑤ Ⓥ | |
| | ✓ ✓ ✓ <u>bear</u> ✓ ✓<br>      best | 1 | | M S Ⓥ | |

**How the Child Monitored**

**plays**  uses initial and final visual information
**puts**    to monitor (although final visual
may be the result of attention to structure),
but ignores meaning.

**bear**  monitors using initial visual
**best**  information.

**Instructional Implication**

**plays**  **bear**  Both errors show that the
**puts**    **best**  child needs to use meaning
along with the visual information. Using
meaning would probably trigger the child to
reread and would assist with self-correction.

| Text | Running Record | E | SC | E (M S V) | SC (M S V) |
|------|----------------|---|-----|-----------|-----|
| Father bear puts in some yellow bananas. "Bananas are the best!" he said. 4 | ✓ ✓ <u>pulls</u> ✓ ✓<br>   puts | 1 | | M ⑤ Ⓥ | |
| | ✓ <u>bandaids</u><br>  bananas | 1 | | M ⑤ Ⓥ | |
| | <u>Bandaids</u> ✓ ✓ <u>b- e- st</u> ✓ ✓<br>Bananas       best | 2 | | M S Ⓥ<br>M S Ⓥ | |

**How the Child Monitored**

**pulls**  **bandaids**  attends to some visual
**puts**   **bananas**  information including the
initial letter, the vowel, and the -s ending,
but ignores the meaning of the story.

**b-e-st**  is decoded in an isolated fashion
**best**    (b- e- st) and shows the child can
analyze visual information sequentially.
Again, this shows the child's use of visual
information with a lack of monitoring
for meaning.

**Instructional Implication**

The child's error pattern on pages 3 and
4 repeatedly shows attention to visual
information without monitoring for meaning.
The child should be taught to think about
the story and reread as a way to monitor when
something does not make sense. The book
introduction and comments made during the
reading should direct the child's attention to
the meaning of the story and should clearly
identify that the story is about a bear family
making fruit salad.

| Text | Running Record | Count | | Information Used | |
|---|---|---|---|---|---|
| | | E | SC | E M S V | SC M S V |

Sister bear puts in some little grapes.
"Grapes are the best!" she said.

5

✓ ✓ <u>p-✓</u> ✓ ✓ ✓ ✓
     puts

✓ ✓ ✓ ✓ ✓ ✓

### How the Child Monitored

 <u>**p-✓**</u> indicates the child has begun to
**puts** monitor, using some initial visual
information.

### Instructional Implication

The child is demonstrating attention to
multiple sources of information, integrating
meaning, structure, and visual information.

# WHO'S DOING THE MONITORING?

When taking a running record, you are not allowed to interrupt the student to do any teaching—and that's a good thing! It guarantees the child gets the wait time needed to notice errors and correct them. And it gives us an opportunity to see if and how the child engages in monitoring behavior. As tempting as it may be, do not teach during the running record!

It is equally important to give a student wait time during reading instruction. As you listen to each student read a page or two, record errors and self-corrections. Take notes on his or her fluency, comments, and behaviors. When the child makes an error, pause, observe, and give him or her time to notice and fix the error. Avoid jumping in immediately. Wait until the child finishes the sentence or paragraph before you prompt. Ask yourself, "Who's doing the monitoring?", because it is common to monitor for children without realizing it. If you are the one noticing and pointing out the errors, the child will become dependent on you and wait for you to do the work, which, of course, can lead to a passive approach to reading.

If a child is passive, that will also influence the running record because if he is dependent on you, he has no option but to appeal for help during the reading and likely receive a Told from you. Monitoring is an independent behavior and must be initiated by the child. It is a mechanism that signals action on his or her part. When you wait and allow the child to monitor on his or her own, it promotes independence. When you monitor for the student, you may think you're being helpful, but you actually may be hindering his or her ability to problem-solve independently.

## Recognizing and Valuing Monitoring

If the child fails to monitor, wait until she finishes the sentence or page, and then prompt her to return to where the error occurred and reread. If the child fails to monitor and keeps on reading, it is helpful to know what to say to encourage the necessary monitoring and self-correction. In the chart on the next page, we provide several "if – then" examples to assist you.

**PART III**

| If the child... | Say... |
|---|---|
| inserts or omits words<br><br>makes up or invents the text | "Try that again. Did what you say match what you see?"<br><br>"Were there too many words?"<br><br>"Did you have enough words?" |
| ignores or misreads a known word | "Show me the word *was*. Now read that sentence again."<br><br>"This word is tricking you. Write it on the whiteboard." Engaging in the motor movement of writing a word will often trigger memory of the word. |
| substitutes a word that makes sense but has no visual similarity (e.g., the child reads *horse* for *pony*) | "Something didn't look right on this page. Can you find it?"<br><br>"What letters would you expect to see at the beginning of *horse*? Is that what you see?"<br><br>"Are you right? Check that word with your finger. Does it look like *horse*?" |
| substitutes a word that doesn't make sense (e.g., the child reads *road* for *grass*, which doesn't make sense at the sentence level or within the overall meaning of the text) | "Are you right?"<br><br>"Something didn't make sense when you read this page. Can you find it?"<br><br>"Read this again, think about what is happening in the story, and use the letters to help you. Remember, it has to make sense and look right." |
| substitutes a word that doesn't fit grammatically or structurally, based on standard English (e.g., the child reads *bear* for *best*) | "Read this again and listen to yourself. Is that how it sounds in a book? Use the letters to help you." |

Monitoring behaviors appear in many forms. Sometimes the behavior is obvious, and at other times it is hard to detect. Therefore, we must always closely observe children to see how and when they're monitoring. In the chart below, we provide several "if – then" examples for when children monitor during reading.

| If the Child Monitors, Say | |
| --- | --- |
| **If the child...** | **Say...** |
| stops, shakes his head, or says something that signals that he knows he isn't right and doesn't know what to do to fix the error | "You noticed something! That is what readers do!" (Values monitoring and reinforces its importance.)<br><br>"Why did you stop? What did you notice?" (Values monitoring and provides insight into the child's processing.) |
| hesitates and then reads the word correctly | "Were you right? How did you know?" (Values and reinforces monitoring and encourages searching and confirming behaviors—children must know when they are right and when they are wrong!) |
| hesitates and then reads the word incorrectly | "Were you right? What letters would you expect to see at the beginning (middle) (end)?" "Check it. Does it look right? Does it make sense? Would we say it that way in a book?" (Values and reinforces monitoring and encourages further visual and other searching and confirming behaviors.) |

## HOW MONITORING BEHAVIORS APPEAR
## ON THE RUNNING RECORD

When taking a running record, look for signs of uncertainty—both verbal signs (e.g., the child says, "That's not right.") and nonverbal signs (e.g., the child shakes her head, takes her eyes off the print). Note those behaviors in the margin of the record so that you have evidence of where and how the child monitored. Some behaviors, such as stopping and taking no action, appealing for help, rereading, and engaging in further visual analysis, are part of the standard coding system, so note-taking may not be necessary (see Chapter 3).

Self-correcting clearly shows us that the child is monitoring. She has expressed dissatisfaction with the first attempt and knows something is wrong. Once the child has monitored, she searches other sources of information to achieve a correct response.

## MONITORING ON VISUAL ASPECTS OF PRINT

Children monitor with aspects of visual information in print, and their monitoring becomes more detailed and sophisticated as they progress. In this section, we show how children's use of visual information changes over time, from simple to complex.

### Monitoring Using One-to-One Correspondence

One of the earliest signs of monitoring is when the student realizes he is reading too many or too few words. One-to-one correspondence is the matching of voice to print, which means a child says one word for each word on the page. It also means the child understands such concepts as left-to-right directional movement, top-to-bottom progression, and the return sweep at the end of a line of print. This voice-to-print match reveals a phonological understanding that in text, the stream of speech is separated by words and spaces. Monitoring using one-to-one correspondence signals a child is attending to print. Over time, he must do it automatically to be free to attend to other aspects of reading. In the following chart, we give examples of three children who read the same page but showed different understandings of one-to-one correspondence.

| Text | Running Record | Explanation |
|---|---|---|
|  This is the bear family. They are making fruit salad. 2 | **Child 1:**<br><br>✓ ✓ ✓ ✓ ✓<br><br>✓ ✓ ✓ $\underline{a}$ ✓ ✓<br>$\quad\quad\quad -$<br><br>Child shakes his head and says, "There's no a!" | The child is monitoring one-to-one, and while he inserts the word *a*, his comment shows that he noticed it was not in the text. |
|  This is the bear family. They are making fruit salad. 2 | **Child 2:**<br><br>$\underline{\text{Here}}$ $\underline{\text{are}}$ ✓ $\underline{\text{four}}$ $\underline{\text{bears}}$<br>$\overline{\text{This}}$ $\overline{\text{is}}$ $\overline{\text{bear}}$ $\overline{\text{family}}$<br><br>✓ $\underline{\text{can}}$ $\underline{\text{make}}$ ✓ ✓<br>$\overline{\text{are}}$ $\overline{\text{making}}$ | The child is monitoring one-to-one in spite of the substitutions. The child pointed to each word as he was saying it and while he is maintaining meaning, the child is using no letter-sound information. Children must first learn to attend to print, and in this example, the child is demonstrating many concepts of print, including that print carries the message. He is also controlling left-to-right directional movement and return sweep. |
|  This is the bear family. They are making fruit salad. 2 | **Child 3:**<br><br>✓ ✓ ✓ $\underline{\text{bears}}$ $\quad -$<br>$\quad\quad\quad\quad \overline{\text{bear}}$ $\overline{\text{family}}$<br><br>✓ ✓ ✓ ✓ ✓ $\underline{\text{with}}$ $\underline{\text{apples}}$<br>$\quad\quad\quad\quad\quad\quad\quad - \quad\quad -$ | As evidenced by the omissions and insertions, the child is not monitoring on one-to-one. |

### *Teaching Students to Monitor Using One-to-One Correspondence*

The following examples show ways to teach one-to-one correspondence during individual, small-group, and whole-group instruction, and during independent practice.

### Individual Instruction

- Line up three to four objects, such as small toys or colored blocks, and put a space between each one. Have the child point to and name each item.

- On a strip of paper, write a simple sentence that contains the child's name and another known word or two—for example, *Austin can jump.* Then cut the sentence into individual words and exaggerate the spacing between them. Have the child point to each word as he reads the sentence. Reduce the amount of space between the words, and have the child read the sentence again.

# Austin    can    jump.

- Choose a simple sentence from a book, and have the child use his index fingers to frame each word as he reads the sentence. Isolating each word builds awareness of the space between each word as he moves across a line of text.

- While the child is reading, use prompts from the charts on pages 117–118.

## Small-Group Instruction

- If you have a group of children who are not monitoring using one-to-one correspondence, select books that have a single line of print on each page, an easy-to-read font, and a generous amount of space between each word. Preferably, the picture and print will be on separate pages to reduce distraction, which will help the children pay attention to the words, and help you remain focused on where each child is looking.

- Have the children use fun pointers, such as Martian fingers, colored craft sticks, or chopsticks to point to each word as they read. There are lots of commercial options, but pointers are easy to make, too.

- Have the children count the words in a sentence to help them identify and track each word.

- While the children are reading, use prompts in the charts on pages 117–118.

## Whole-Group Instruction

- Teach one-to-one correspondence during shared reading. Call on children who need extra help with one-to-one correspondence to track the print in the displayed text (e.g., big book, poem, song, nursery rhyme, or a text created during interactive or shared writing), using a long pointer. Provide hand-over-hand assistance at the chart and use prompts that appear in the charts on pages 117–118, as needed.

- During interactive or shared writing, clap the number of words in the sentence you are writing together and draw a corresponding line for each word.

- During interactive or shared writing, after writing a sentence together on chart paper, have a child use two fingers to mark the spaces between the words. Children who have trouble with one-to-one correspondence typically also have trouble with word boundaries. This activity builds awareness that there has to be a match between what is said and what appears on the chart.

<u>Our</u>  <u>class</u>  <u>reads</u>  <u>books</u>  <u>for</u>  <u>fun.</u>

## Independent Practice

- Make pointers available for children to use during independent practice. They can use the pointers as they reread books and charts you've read together during shared reading and interactive or shared writing.

- Make books available for children to read that contain their names and simple sentences (e.g., *Griff can run. Griff can hop.*).

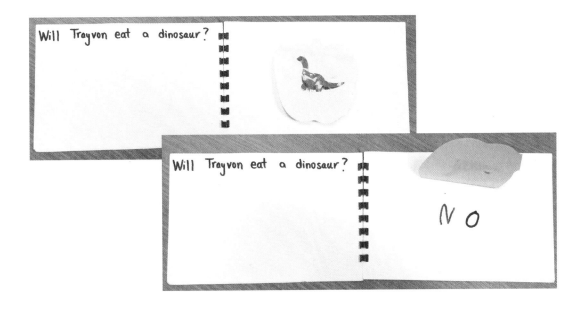

## Monitoring Using Known Words

Known words are words a child can read and write automatically. They serve as an anchor in print and help the child monitor on one-to-one correspondence. For example, a child who knows the word *can* should read that word when it appears in the text and should not substitute it for another word. The number of known words children need to use to monitor should increase over time. Children use known words to keep themselves on track. In the following chart, we give examples of how two children use known words to help them monitor their reading.

| Text | Running Record | Explanation |
|---|---|---|
| 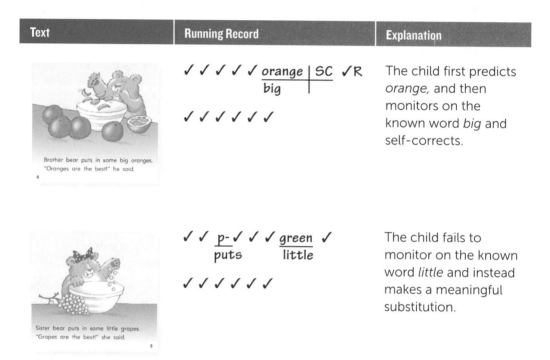 Brother bear puts in some big oranges. "Oranges are the best!" he said. 6 | ✓ ✓ ✓ ✓ ✓ orange \| SC ✓R<br>           big<br>✓ ✓ ✓ ✓ ✓ ✓ | The child first predicts *orange,* and then monitors on the known word *big* and self-corrects. |
| Sister bear puts in some little grapes. "Grapes are the best!" she said. 5 | ✓ ✓ p-✓ ✓ ✓ green ✓<br>    puts        little<br>✓ ✓ ✓ ✓ ✓ ✓ | The child fails to monitor on the known word *little* and instead makes a meaningful substitution. |

## Teaching Students to Monitor Using Known Words

The following examples show ways to increase children's known words during individual, small-group, and whole-group instruction and during independent practice.

### Individual Instruction

- Have the child use her index fingers to frame known words in a text. Also, offer multisensory opportunities for the child to work with known words by having her trace or write words or make them with magnetic letters.

- Use a masking card to isolate individual words in a text, and have the child read the words. Children need to read high-frequency words quickly and accurately.

- Use flash cards to review words.
- If a child reads a known word incorrectly, prompt her to reread the page or sentence that contains the word. Say, "Something didn't look right. Reread this." If the child reads the word incorrectly again, place a finger above the known word and tap it to draw her attention to it.
- While the child is reading, use prompts from the charts on pages 117–118.

### Small-Group Instruction

- The suggestions for individual instruction also work for small-group instruction.
- Give children lots of practice with words so they can read them automatically when they encounter them in a text. Devote special attention and provide extra practice with words that are visually similar (e.g., *will, with / they, them, then, there / don't, didn't / want, went, wanted / what, when, why, who*). Provide a variety of materials for working on known words, such as sandpaper, Magna Doodles, Boogie Boards™, gel boards, water pens, chalk, and scented markers.

### Whole-Group Instruction

- During shared reading, invite the children to find and frame known words in an enlarged text (e.g., a big book, digital book, poem, song, or text created during interactive or shared writing).
- During interactive or shared writing, have children write known words on the chart. While one child is at the chart, have the other children write the words on individual dry-erase boards or on the floor with their finger.

### Independent Practice

- Have an individualized list of words for each child to practice at a word study center. Make a variety of materials available for children to write and/or construct words (e.g., letter stamps, magnetic letters, old keyboards, Magna Doodles, gel pens).

| am | before | said |
| can | couldn't | there |
| go | new | they |
| here | want | was |
| is | wanted | when |
| to | would | where |

## Key Terms

**Alphabetic Principle** The correspondence between letters and sounds

**Decoding** Using letters and sounds to read words—may include sounding out a word, decoding by analogy (using knowledge of similar words), breaking apart words by onsets and rimes (*fr-ight*), syllables (*re-mem-ber*), and by prefixes, suffixes, and roots (*dis-courage-ment*)

**Encoding** Translating spoken sounds into written letters—as required in spelling out words—the opposite of decoding

**Morpheme** The smallest unit of meaning in language (e.g., *read* – one morpheme; *reading*—two morphemes)

**Orthography** The spelling system

**Phoneme** The smallest unit of sound in language (e.g., *shark* has three phonemes: /sh/ /ar/ /k/.)

**Phonics** An approach to teaching reading that focuses on letter-sound relationships and patterns as a way to support efficient word recognition

**Phonogram** The letter or letter cluster that represents a phoneme. A phonogram (also known as a grapheme) may consist of one or more letters; for example, the long-*i* sound in *night* is represented by *-igh: n-igh-t.*

# Monitoring Using Detailed Visual Information

Detailed visual information refers to letters, sounds, and orthographic patterns. When children decode, they use detailed visual information to solve unknown words. Children may try to decode words letter by letter, but that is not the most productive method. Instead, they should use the largest and most efficient units of visual information in the word. When taking a running record, note the types of detailed visual information on which the child monitors, including beginning letters, blends, digraphs, *r*-controlled vowels, vowel combinations, endings, and phonograms. As children develop as readers, their use of detailed visual information becomes more sophisticated and includes syllables and morphological units. In the following chart, we give examples of how three children monitored, or failed to monitor, for detailed visual information.

| Text | Running Record | Explanation |
|---|---|---|
| Mother bear puts in some red apples. "Apples are the best!" she said. 3 | Mom ✓ cuts⊙✓ ✓ ✓<br>Mother puts<br><br>✓ ✓ ✓ ✓ ✓ ✓ | The child substitutes *Mom* for *Mother*, monitoring with beginning letter/sound information. The child substitutes *cuts* for *puts*, monitoring some visual information (*-uts*), but ignores the initial visual information. |
| Sister bear puts in some little grapes. "Grapes are the best!" she said. 5 | ✓ ✓ p-✓ ✓ ✓ ✓ ✓<br>puts<br><br>✓ ✓ ✓ ✓ ✓ ✓ | The child articulates /p/ before saying *puts*, monitoring with first-letter visual information. |
| Baby bear has a job, too. He mixes up the fruit salad. 7 | ✓ ✓ had ✓ ✓ ✓<br>has<br><br>✓ stirs ✓ ✓ ✓ ✓<br>mixes | The child says *had* for *has*, monitoring with initial visual information, but ignored ending visual information. The child says *stirs* for *mixes*, showing the child is not monitoring any visual information. |

### *Teaching Students to Monitor Using Detailed Visual Information*

The following examples show ways to teach children to monitor using visual information during individual, small-group, and whole-group instruction, and during independent practice.

PART III

### Individual Instruction

- Use an alphabet book to personalize the child's letter-sound links by having him select a picture to represent a letter sound. Include the letters and picture/sound links that the child knows, adding as his repertoire grows.

- While saying the word slowly, have the child run his finger under the word in question to check if the letters he sees match the sounds he's making. This reinforces monitoring and helps the child determine if he is right or wrong.

- While the child is reading, use the prompts in the charts on pages 117 and 118.

### Small-Group Instruction

- After they've finished reading, ask students to follow along in their books as you read a sentence aloud. Make an error on a word that is visually similar to the word in the book, such as *mom* for *mother*, or *started* for *stayed*. Say, "Find my mistake. Let's check the word by saying it slowly while we run a finger under it."

- During word study, use the Making Words activity described in *The Next Step Forward in Guided Reading* (Richardson, 2016) and *The Next Step Forward in Word Study and Phonics* (Richardson & Dufresne, 2019). Students use magnetic letters to make a series of words that differ by one or two letters (e.g., *trim-trip-strip-strap*).

  - Give students the letters they need to make all the words in the series, and then dictate the first word for them to make (e.g., *trim*). After they make the word, teach them to check the word by saying it slowly as they run their finger under the letters.

  - Then dictate the next word (e.g., *trip*). Before they make the letter change, have them say the new word as they run their finger under the previous word. This action helps them coordinate their auditory- and visual-processing speeds and notice the letter(s) they need to change. They will use the same process to monitor for visual information and self-correct during reading. After they make the new word, continue the activity by dictating the other words in the sequence.

This engaging activity teaches children how to use sounds to monitor for visual information during reading and writing. It also strengthens left-to-right visual scanning across a word.

## Whole-Group Instruction

- During interactive and shared writing, post and refer to an alphabet chart with corresponding key pictures to reinforce the alphabetic principle.

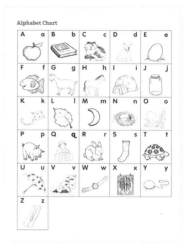

- Create a name chart to explore the letter-sound relationships in children's names. Link their names to words with similar features to give them practice in checking for visual detail (e.g., *Nash* begins the same as *Noah*; Piper's name ends the same as *her* or *faster*).

- Create a word wall organized by vowel patterns (*ar, ay, oa,* etc.). With the children's help, select a key word to post for each pattern (*car, day, boat,* etc.) Then refer to the word wall during interactive and shared writing to check and confirm that words you want to use are spelled correctly (e.g., "Let's use *car* on our key word wall to check the spelling of *start*").

- Use a cloze procedure in which children read a sentence that contains intentionally deleted words and generate words that would fit. For example, for "My dad likes to cook _____," children may suggest pizza, hot dogs, hamburgers, ham, steak, tacos, soup, and mac and cheese. You then reveal the first letter (e.g., *h*), which narrows the word options and requires the children to use beginning visual information to confirm. Next, reveal more letters (e.g., *h- am*). In most cases, this should not be done letter by letter but instead should reveal units of information to support decoding efforts (e.g., rimes, *r*-controlled vowels, vowel combinations). Based on the visual information, the children narrow the options on the list further (e.g., *ham* or *hamburger*). This activity helps children thoroughly check words, supporting the use of visual information while maintaining meaning.

- Use word ladders, which require students to create new words from a known word by systematically changing one letter or multiple letters. There are published options, or you can make your own word ladders.

### Independent Practice

- For a word study center, create a word strip that children can use to make words by changing the onset and retaining the rime (e.g., *r-at, ch-at, th-at*) or by retaining the onset and changing the rime (e.g., *step-stop*).

- Provide students with picture cards and magnetic letters. Then have them use the letters to make the words of images pictured on the cards. If you write the word on the back of each card, students can self-check their work.

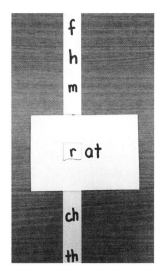

# MONITORING USING MEANING

Monitoring using meaning occurs when a child is guided by his understanding of the text. A child's ability to monitor for meaning depends largely on his background knowledge about the topic, the size of his vocabulary, and/or his familiarity with characters and other text elements. When children are monitoring using meaning, they are checking to see if what they are reading makes sense. Because children are meaning makers, this information source keeps them on track as they read, serving as both a feed-forward and feedback mechanism. The feed-forward process (Clay, 2001) helps students make meaningful attempts on unknown words. The feedback process is at work when students notice that what they say makes sense but doesn't match the visual information. In the chart below, we give examples of children who do and do not monitor using meaning.

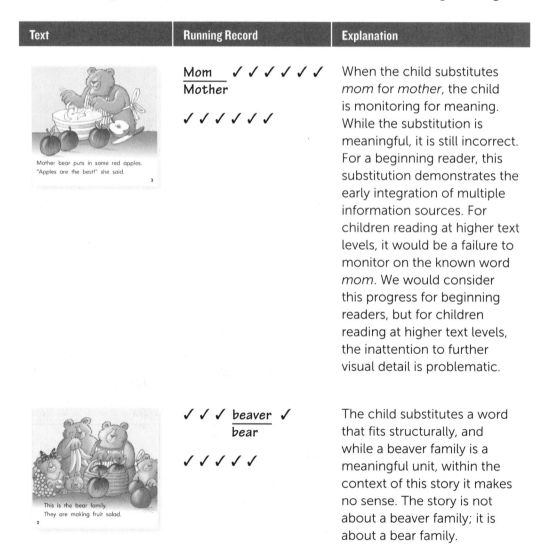

| Text | Running Record | Explanation |
| --- | --- | --- |
| Mother bear puts in some red apples. "Apples are the best!" she said. 3 | Mom ✓ ✓ ✓ ✓ ✓ / Mother <br><br> ✓ ✓ ✓ ✓ ✓ | When the child substitutes *mom* for *mother*, the child is monitoring for meaning. While the substitution is meaningful, it is still incorrect. For a beginning reader, this substitution demonstrates the early integration of multiple information sources. For children reading at higher text levels, it would be a failure to monitor on the known word *mom*. We would consider this progress for beginning readers, but for children reading at higher text levels, the inattention to further visual detail is problematic. |
| This is the bear family. They are making fruit salad. 2 | ✓ ✓ ✓ *beaver* ✓ / bear <br><br> ✓ ✓ ✓ ✓ ✓ | The child substitutes a word that fits structurally, and while a beaver family is a meaningful unit, within the context of this story it makes no sense. The story is not about a beaver family; it is about a bear family. |

*Teaching Students to Monitor Using Meaning*

The following examples show different ways to teach children to monitor using meaning during individual, small-group, and whole-group instruction, and during independent practice.

## Individual Instruction

- Select books that have familiar content and vocabulary (informational) or characters, story lines, and other text elements (narrative).

- Tailor your book introduction to support meaning-making. Have the child discuss the illustrations to build a foundation for comprehension.

- As the child reads, prompt her to focus on meaning, primarily when she turns the page. Your prompts should be quick and to the point (e.g., "What fruit will go in the salad next?").

- As the child reads, also use the charts on pages 117–118 to prompt monitoring for meaning.

## Small-Group Instruction

- After the reading, engage children in conversation to extend their thinking about the text (retell the sequence events, identify the problem and solution, generate alternative endings, infer a character's feelings). Chart the children's collaborative responses during an interactive or shared writing session. Children can also respond individually by drawing or writing in a response journal.

- After the reading, ask students to follow along in their books as you read a sentence aloud. Deliberately make an error that does not make sense. Ask, "Did that make sense? Find my mistake. If what you're reading doesn't make sense, always reread and fix it."

## Whole-Group Instruction

- For read-alouds, choose books that are culturally responsive and expose children to a range of genres and topics. This extends vocabulary and builds background knowledge. Texts used for read-alouds should expose students to complex literary language and structures.

## Independent Practice

- Create time in the day for independent reading. Be sure your classroom library is stocked with a variety of books that are appealing to all your students.

- Encourage students to reread books they have read during small-group instruction, on their own or with a partner. This builds fluency and comprehension.

# MONITORING USING STRUCTURE AND LANGUAGE

Children's everyday oral language (e.g., language used on the playground or at home with a sibling) may not directly match the structure and language in the text. Further, if a student is learning English as a second language or uses a regional dialect, he may not be aware that his errors do not match the text. For example, if a child says *comed* for *came*, he is using a standard English rule to recognize a word's past tense but isn't using standard English structure. It is important to value children's everyday language and view it as a rich resource and as a starting point for engagement with text. Eventually children will come to understand that language varies depending on content and context. Exposure to language in a variety of settings, as well as hearing and using language in conversation, is critical. Once children have heard language and structure associated with text, and have used them in their oral language, they can begin to use them to monitor their reading. When reading, meaning and structure are often linked, which is why errors in a running record are usually coded for both meaning and structure. In the chart below, we give examples of how a child monitored and failed to monitor using language and structure.

| Text | Running Record | Explanation |
|---|---|---|
| 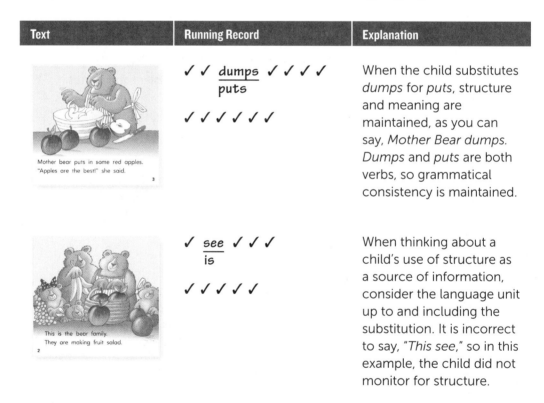Mother bear puts in some red apples. "Apples are the best!" she said. 3 | ✓ ✓ $\underline{\text{dumps}}$ ✓ ✓ ✓ ✓<br>    puts<br><br>✓ ✓ ✓ ✓ ✓ | When the child substitutes *dumps* for *puts*, structure and meaning are maintained, as you can say, *Mother Bear dumps. Dumps* and *puts* are both verbs, so grammatical consistency is maintained. |
| This is the bear family. They are making fruit salad. 2 | ✓ $\underline{\text{see}}$ ✓ ✓ ✓<br>  is<br><br>✓ ✓ ✓ ✓ ✓ | When thinking about a child's use of structure as a source of information, consider the language unit up to and including the substitution. It is incorrect to say, "*This see*," so in this example, the child did not monitor for structure. |

### *Teaching Students to Monitor Using Language and Structure*

The following examples show different ways to teach children to monitor using language and structure during individual, small-group, and whole-group instruction, and during independent practice.

#### Individual Instruction

- Before the student reads, rehearse phrases and sentences that contain unusual or unfamiliar structures, even if the the words are known. For example, the child may know each word in the phrase *So can I,* but he may be unfamiliar with the phrase's structure, so it should be rehearsed.

- As the child reads, use the charts on pages 117–118 to prompt him to monitor for structure.

#### Small-Group Instruction

- Select books that contain language structures that are close to the language children would normally use. For example, it is not unusual for children to be able to read, *A dog is here,* but have trouble with *Here is a dog* because of the way it is structured. Avoid books with uncommon or awkward structures (e.g., *Find me a dog to play with me. Find me a cat to stay with me.*). Sometimes it is helpful to ask yourself, "Would a child say it that way?"

- Use interactive and shared writing to introduce children to different ways to express an idea. Specifically, reframe a sentence structurally while maintaining meaning (e.g., *"We go to recess after lunch"* becomes *"After lunch, we go to recess."*) Doing that adds variety to your writing charts and exposes children to the variety of ways a single idea can be structured.

### Whole-Group Instruction

- Select a variety of books to read aloud that expose children to complex literary language and structures. Choose narrative texts that contain dialogue and informational texts that contain content-specific language.

- Read poems and songs during shared reading. Their rhyme, rhythm, and repetition help students assimilate unfamiliar structures into their everyday language.

- Display a picture. Then use interactive or shared writing to describe the picture, using different sentence structures. For example, a picture of a bear walking through the forest could be described in the following ways:

  - *The big, brown bear is walking through the forest.*

  - *In the middle of the forest, a bear is walking in search of something to eat.*

### Independent Practice

- Create time in the day for independent reading. Create a comfortable place for children to read. Stock your classroom library with a variety of books that are appealing to your students and match their current independent reading levels.

- Encourage students to read books with a partner. Pair students learning English with students who have strong control of English.

## CLOSING THOUGHT

Monitoring is a critical reading skill. Children must learn to monitor to make sure whatever they're reading makes sense, is structurally acceptable, and looks right based on the letters they see and the sounds those letters produce. The goal is always accurate reading. Readers who fail to monitor cannot engage in the problem solving needed to move from partially correct responding to accurate and automatic reading. Running records help us observe and document monitoring so that we can modify and differentiate our teaching to help young readers become proficient.

# CHAPTER 8

# Understanding Student Appeals for Help and Teacher "Tolds"

Sometimes it is necessary for us to intervene while taking a running record to give the child the correct word. This is referred to as a "Told." In this chapter, we discuss various types of Tolds, when it makes sense to give them, and the benefits and consequences of giving them.

The chart on the following pages captures a child's reading of *Frogs and Toads Are Cool Creatures* by Megan Duhamel (Level J). Examine it and think about the Tolds the child received. Use the following questions to guide your thinking.

- Were all Tolds necessary?
- What did the child do to try and figure out the word before receiving the Told?
- Is there a particular type of word for which the Tolds are given?
- Aside from the Tolds, what other thoughts do I have about the child's reading of this text?

| Text | Running Record | Count | | Information Used | |
|---|---|---|---|---|---|
| | | E | SC | E<br>M S V | SC<br>M S V |

Let's start with frogs. Frogs spend some time in water and some time on land. Frogs breathe through their noses. But they also breathe through their skin when they are in the water.

✓ ✓ ✓ ✓ ✓ ✓ ✓

✓ ✓ ✓ ✓ ✓ ✓ ✓

$\dfrac{\text{br- eat- he} | A | \ \ |R}{\text{breathe} \ \ | \ \ | T |}$ ✓ ✓ ✓ ✓ ✓    1        M S Ⓥ

✓ ✓ ✓ ✓ ✓ ✓ ✓

✓ ✓ ✓

There are 4,000 kinds of frogs. There are big frogs. This bullfrog weighs more than a baseball.

✓ ✓ ✓ ✓ ✓ ✓ ✓

✓ ✓ ✓ ✓ $\dfrac{\text{we – weg} |}{\text{weighs} \ \ | T}$ ✓ ✓    1        M S Ⓥ

✓ ✓

There are little frogs. This tree frog is the size of a dime. It has little sticky pads on its feet. A tree frog's special feet help it climb straight up a window.

✓ ✓ ✓ ✓ ✓ ✓ ✓ ✓

✓ ✓ ✓ ✓ ✓ ✓ ✓ ✓ ✓

✓ ✓ ✓ ✓ ✓ ✓ ✓ ✓

✓ $\dfrac{\text{str- ight} |}{\text{straight} | T}$ ✓ ✓ ✓    1        M S Ⓥ

| Text | Running Record | Count | | Information Used | |
|---|---|---|---|---|---|
| | | **E** | **SC** | **E**<br>**M S V** | **SC**<br>**M S V** |
| There are brightly colored frogs. This dart frog's bright colors warn predators not to mess with it. It is poisonous! | ✓ ✓ ✓ ✓ ✓ ✓ <br> ✓ ✓ ✓ <br> pre- dat- ors │A│ ✓ ✓ <br> predators │ │T | 1 | | M S Ⓥ | |
| | ✓ ✓ ✓ ✓ ✓ po- is- on -us│ <br> poisonous │T | 1 | | M S Ⓥ | |
| Toads are also interesting. They are similar to frogs in many ways. Toads have big, bulging eyes and long, sticky tongues. Like frogs, toads hop and eat bugs. | ✓ ✓ ✓ ✓ ✓ ✓ <br> ✓ ✓ ✓ ✓ ✓ ✓ ✓ <br> bull – ging│ ✓ ✓ ✓ ✓ ✓ <br> bulging │T <br> ✓ ✓ ✓ ✓ ✓ ✓ | 1 | | M S Ⓥ | |
| But toads are different from frogs, too. Toads do not live in water. They live only on land. Toads also have fatter bodies and dryer, rougher skin. | ✓ ✓ ✓ ✓ ✓ ✓ <br> ✓ ✓ ✓ ✓ ✓ ✓ ✓ ✓ <br> ✓ ✓ ✓ ✓ ✓ ✓ ✓ <br> ✓ r- ou- her│ ✓ <br> rougher │T | 1 | | M S Ⓥ | |

PART III

| Text | Running Record | Count | | Information Used | |
|------|----------------|-------|---|------------------|---|
| | | E | SC | E<br>M S V | SC<br>M S V |

**Your Thoughts**

**Guiding Questions**

- Were all Tolds necessary?
- What did the child do to try to figure out the word before receiving the Told?
- Is there a type of word for which the Tolds are given?
- Aside from the Tolds, what other thoughts do I have about the child's reading of this text?

**Our Thoughts**

The teacher may be giving the Tolds too quickly. In five of the seven Tolds, the child was working on the word and did not appeal for help. Perhaps if the teacher had given more wait time, the child would have solved the word. Because the teacher told the student the word, we do not know what actions the child might have taken. Perhaps the child would have used meaning to self-correct the word. This teacher needs to provide more wait time and only provide a Told if the child appeals or takes no action. The teacher also needs to teach the student to search for more visual information, integrating decoding attempts with meaning. Word study on vowel patterns is warranted. For the most part, the child is engaged in accurate reading and, on the words that are given as Tolds, the child always makes an attempt before appealing for help. For example when the child comes to *weigh*, he first reads *we* (long *e*). Sometimes this happens when children are instructed to find the little word in the big word. While this works in isolated cases, it also presents problems. On the child's second attempt, he reads *weg*. While the child had made two attempts searching and using more visual information each time, he does not use the larger unit, in this case, *eight*. The child fails to break at the onset and rime (*w-eight*) and does not recognize the known number word (*eight*).

Tolds should be given sparingly, even if you think you have a good reason to give one. Otherwise, you risk the child habitually appealing at the point of difficulty, instead of engaging in problem-solving behavior. Appealing for help can be a hard habit to break and leads to the child approaching print passively rather than actively.

## TYPES OF TOLDS

Tolds are given for various reasons. The chart below categorizes Tolds by type and gives an example and explanation of each one.

| Type | Example | Explanation |
|---|---|---|
| **Preempting Told**  <br><br> **The child makes a substitution that is repeated throughout the text, and the teacher gives a Told.** | In the book *Danny Helps Dad*, the word *helps* is repeated five times in the text. The child reads *lets* for *helps* the first time it appears. The teacher gives the child a Told so the student would not make an error on the word later in the text. <br><br>  <br> Danny helps Dad clean the house. "I will pick up the toys," said Danny. | Although the reader uses meaning and structure when reading *lets* for *helps*, she neglects the visual information. The teacher should not have given a Told because there was no appeal from the child or stop after the error. The teacher knew the word would appear later in the text and probably gave the Told to improve the accuracy rate. Giving the Told robbed the child of an opportunity to monitor with visual information and potentially self-correct when the word appeared again. |

| Type | Example | Explanation |
|---|---|---|

**Correcting Told**

The child makes a meaningful substitution on a word, and the teacher gives a Told.

In the book *How to Make Pizza*, the sentence is *The man puts on some spices*. The child reads *salts* for *spices* and shows no hesitation but the teacher interrupts and gives a Told.

The man puts on some spices.
Now the pizza is ready to go in the oven.

9

The child's attempt is meaningful but matches only the first and last letters in the word. By correcting the child and telling the word, the teacher loses a teaching opportunity. If the teacher had refrained from the Told, she could have come back to this example after the text was completed. The teacher could have asked the child to find the error to demonstrate monitoring and self-correcting behaviors.

**Rescuing Told**

The child comes to a difficult word and before doing any work, the teacher gives a Told.

In the book *Bird's New Nest*, the sentence is, *The sticks are too sharp*. The child is reading along fluently, comes to *sharp*, and pauses momentarily. Before the child can take any action, the teacher gives the child the word.

Bird sits on the sticks.
Does Bird like the sticks?
No. The sticks are too sharp.

4

Generally, these types of Tolds indicate that the teacher expects the child to misread. The teacher tells the word to rescue the student from failure. This limits the opportunity for the student to problem-solve.

| Type | Example | Explanation |
|---|---|---|

**Interrupting Told**

The child is working on the word, but the teacher jumps in and gives a Told.

In the book *Bird's New Nest*, the sentence is, *The sticks are too sharp*. The child is reading along fluently and pauses at the word sharp. The child says /sh/, /sh/, and before the child can take any other action, the teacher tells the word.

Bird sits on the sticks.
Does Bird like the sticks?
No. The sticks are too sharp.

When a child is working on a word, it is important not to give a Told. Give the child time to problem-solve. Record the child's actions. Perhaps the child would have reread to gather more meaning or she could have continued to search for more visual information. The teacher should not interrupt the child's processing.

**Balking Told**

The child stops and refuses to take action, and the teacher gives a Told.

In the book *Danny Helps Dad*, the child stops at the word *helps* and does not try to solve the word.

Danny helps Dad clean the house.
"I will pick up the toys," said Danny.

If the child stops and appeals for help, the teacher can say, "You try it." But if there is no verbal appeal, a Told is given. While the Told is necessary, the instructional implications are critical. The teacher must analyze the child's behavior to understand why the child refuses to take action. Is there a particular type of word that challenges the reader? The teacher should use this information to inform her teaching decisions and demonstrate to the child what to do when encountering an unknown word.

| Type | Example | Explanation |
|---|---|---|
| **Generating**<br>Told<br><br>**The child has worked on the word and exhausted his options, and the teacher gives a Told.** | In the book *The Lemonade Stand*, the sentence is, *It is too hot to do anything*. The child pauses at *anything* and says *an* and then rereads, unable to read the bigger part *any*. The child says *an* again, reads *thing*, and then says *nothing* for *anything*. It is apparent from the child's behavior that he is not satisfied with his response and refuses to continue reading.<br> | The child tried multiple ways to solve the word. His refusal to go on signaled to the teacher that a Told was necessary. Even though a Told was given, recording the work the child did provides great insight into the child's processing. |

Being aware of the various types of Tolds helps us understand *our* behavior while taking a running record, as well as during instruction. If giving Tolds is something you do with all children frequently, you need to check your behavior. Here are some ways to determine if you may be giving too many Tolds:

- Look across running records you have taken on your students. How many "T"s do you see?

- Are you giving Tolds to all students, or just the students who truly benefit from them?

- Using the charts on pages 141–144, identify the type(s) of Tolds you are giving. Once you've done that, reflect on why you may be giving them, whether they are appropriate, and how you can change your behavior.

- Check on the amount of wait time you are giving children. Are you giving enough for children to problem-solve on their own?

- Are you demonstrating the actions a child should take when he or she comes to an unknown word? This can stop Tolds before they happen!

- Review a series of running records that you took over a few weeks. Is the number of Tolds decreasing?

## ANALYZING THE TYPES OF WORDS THAT ARE TOLD

If you find you are giving Tolds regularly to specific children, it is important to pinpoint the types of words you're telling (Fried, 2013). Categorizing the words will help you identify patterns in a child's reading and make instructional decisions. To find patterns in types of words that are told:

- Collect 3-5 running records that you've taken on the child.

- Circle and count the Tolds you gave in each record.

- Categorize the Tolds by type, using the charts on pages 141–144. Are they high-frequency words? Are they words for which the child does not yet have the necessary skills to decode (e.g., digraphs, vowel patterns, endings, etc.)? Are they words that are not in the child's vocabulary? Keep in mind, some words may fit in more than one category.

- Once you've categorized the Tolds, look for patterns.

## FROM PRACTICE TO PROFICIENCY

The chart on the next page provides examples of Tolds given to three children on three running records. Think about these questions as you examine the Tolds.

**High Frequency** Is the Told a high-frequency word?

**Decodable** Does the child lack the skills necessary to decode the word?

**Concepts/Vocabulary** Is the Told given because the child lacks the concept or vocabulary knowledge to read the word?

# Tolds Given to Three Students While Taking Running Records

## Child 1

| Tolds in Running Record 1 | Tolds in Running Record 2 | Tolds in Running Record 3 |
|---|---|---|
| and / said — T | said / shouted — T | paint / painting — T |
| will / went — T | in / on — T | was / wash — T |
| - / Kate — A / T | went / will — T | B- / Ben — A / T |
| - / eyes — T | - / are — T | |
| play / make — T | | |

## Child 2

| Tolds in Running Record 1 | Tolds in Running Record 2 | Tolds in Running Record 3 |
|---|---|---|
| again / against — T | today / tomorrow — T | m-ing / Morning — T |
| - / don't — T | w- / wouldn't — T | w –hat / what — T |
| - / sound — T | upstairs / uphill — T | sh- st / started — T |
| He / Hello — T | | |

## Child 3

| Tolds in Running Record 1 | Tolds in Running Record 2 | Tolds in Running Record 3 |
|---|---|---|
| will / with — T | th- / thunderstorms — T | -et / equality — T |
| - / hairdresser — T | enter / interested — T | slave / slavery — T |
| | - / nearby — T | in- / infection — T |
| | me-sur-ing / measuring — T | |

Next, place the words into the following categories: High Frequency, Decodable, and Concepts/Vocabulary. Remember, a Told can fall into more than one category and is based on what the child knows and can control. For example, some vocabulary words are easy to decode, such as *thunderstorm* in Child 3's second running record, so the word *thunderstorm* could be placed into two categories: Decodable and Concepts/Vocabulary. Once you've sorted the words into categories, count and record the total number of Tolds from all three running records, as well as from each category. Finally, think about the instructional implications for each of the three children. When you're finished, check your work against the answer key at the end of the chapter.

## Child 1

|  | High Frequency | Decodable | Concepts/Vocabulary |
|---|---|---|---|
| **Total # of Tolds:** | Total # of Tolds: | Total # of Tolds: | Total # of Tolds: |
| **Examples** | | | |
| | | | |
| **Instructional Implications** | | | |

## Child 2

| | High Frequency | Decodable | Concepts/Vocabulary |
|---|---|---|---|
| **Total # of Tolds:** | Total # of Tolds: | Total # of Tolds: | Total # of Tolds: |

**Examples**

**Instructional
Implications**

## Child 3

| | High Frequency | Decodable | Concepts/Vocabulary |
|---|---|---|---|
| **Total # of Tolds:** | Total # of Tolds: | Total # of Tolds: | Total # of Tolds: |
| **Examples** | | | |
| | | | |
| **Instructional Implications** | | | |

An answer is key provided at the end of the chapter.

These same categories—High Frequency, Decodable, and Vocabulary/Concepts—can also be used when analyzing the words that children self-correct. Following the same process as outlined above for Tolds will provide you with insight into the type of support children need. If, for example, a child's self-corrected words all fall into the high-frequency category, the child likely does not know high-frequency words as well as he should, and needs more practice with them.

# NEXT STEPS IN INSTRUCTIONAL DECISION MAKING

Record the child's every behavior and action leading up to and after the Told, because they provide evidence of what the child did and, therefore, are valuable in determining next instructional steps.

Remember to allow adequate wait time before giving a Told and impress upon the child that she must take some action before you'll tell her the word. A Told without an attempt, also referred to as a Rescuing Told, gives us no information about what a child is noticing. What children notice, combined with their behaviors and actions, provides a starting point for instruction. For children to notice, we have to give them adequate wait time.

But what does "adequate" mean? One of the most important things for us to learn is how long to wait before giving a Told. Giving one too quickly deprives the child of the opportunity to problem-solve and take action to self-correct. It also robs you of an opportunity to observe the work of the child. Waiting too long can frustrate a child and cause meaning-making to break down. Deciding on just the right amount of wait time is a delicate balancing act that is learned with practice.

After you give a Told, teach the child to take additional action. She should not view a Told as permission to be passive. Instead, she should do something that will help her retain the word. For example, after you give a Told, have the child run a finger under or look carefully at the word to confirm the visual information. To maintain meaning, ask the child to reread the sentence or phrase and put the Told word back into context.

During small-group instruction, other children may feel it is their responsibility to give Tolds, which isn't much different from you doing it, and does not help the child. When you teach children how to take action, there is little need for anyone, teacher and classmates alike, to provide Tolds.

# CLOSING THOUGHT

Tolds are often viewed as a failure on the child's part to take action. However, they should really be viewed as failure on our part: a failure to accept approximations and encourage risk-taking; a failure to teach students how to decode unknown words; a failure to provide sufficient wait time; a failure to introduce words that are not in the child's vocabulary; and a failure to select the right book for instruction.

While our failures may be hard to face, it is important to recognize why we give Tolds. When we analyze the child's behaviors and actions alongside our own, we create opportunities for problem solving. We must convey to children that it is their job to make attempts and implement what we have taught them. Some Tolds are necessary but many are not, and it is imperative that we think hard about why we're giving them.

**Answer key to the practice activity on pages 146–149:**

## Child 1

| | High Frequency | Decodable | Concepts/Vocabulary |
|---|---|---|---|
| **Total # of Tolds:** 12 | Total # of Tolds: 7 | Total # of Tolds: 1 | Total # of Tolds: 4 |
| **Examples** | $\frac{and}{said}$ T | $\frac{paint}{painting}$ T | $\frac{was}{wash}$ T |
| | $\frac{will}{went}$ T | | $\frac{-}{Kate}$ $\frac{A}{T}$ |
| | $\frac{play}{make}$ T | | $\frac{-}{eyes}$ T |
| | $\frac{said}{shouted}$ T | | $\frac{B-}{Ben}$ $\frac{A}{T}$ |
| | $\frac{in}{on}$ T | | |
| | $\frac{went}{will}$ T | | |
| | $\frac{-}{are}$ T | | |
| **Instructional Implications** | Child 1 averaged four Tolds on each running record, which is way too many. Categorizing the Tolds revealed that the majority are high-frequency words. This indicates that the child needs practice with high-frequency words in texts without repeated patterns. Additionally, the child should practice writing the challenging high-frequency words so the words are automatically recognized in print. | | |

## Child 2

| | High Frequency | Decodable | Concepts/Vocabulary |
|---|---|---|---|
| **Total # of Tolds: 10** | Total # of Tolds: 3 | Total # of Tolds: 7 | Total # of Tolds: 0 |
| **Examples** | $\dfrac{-}{don't}$ \| T | $\dfrac{again}{against}$ \| T | |
| | $\dfrac{w\text{-}}{wouldn't}$ \| T | $\dfrac{-}{sound}$ \| T | |
| | $\dfrac{w\text{ -hat}}{what}$ \| T | $\dfrac{He}{Hello}$ \| T | |
| | | $\dfrac{today}{tomorrow}$ \| T | |
| | | $\dfrac{upstairs}{uphill}$ \| T | |
| | | $\dfrac{m\text{-ing}}{Morning}$ \| T | |
| | | $\dfrac{sh\text{- st}}{started}$ \| T | |

**Instructional Implications**

Child 2 averaged three Tolds on each running record, which is too many. By categorizing the Tolds, it is obvious that the majority occur on words the child should be able to decode. For the most part, the child uses some initial letter/sound information to substitute a word from language that may or may not be meaningful. Once the child substitutes the word, he does not confirm his response with more detailed visual information. The child will need to learn how to decode words while making sure they make sense in the text.

## Child 3

| | High Frequency | Decodable | Concepts/Vocabulary |
|---|---|---|---|
| **Total # of Tolds:** 9 | Total # of Tolds: 1 | Total # of Tolds: 2 | Total # of Tolds: 7 |
| **Examples** | $\dfrac{\text{will}}{\text{with}}$ T | $\dfrac{\text{enter}}{\text{interested}}$ T | $\dfrac{\text{-}}{\text{hairdresser}}$ T |
| | | $\dfrac{\text{th-}}{\text{thunderstorms}}$ T | $\dfrac{\text{th-}}{\text{thunderstorms}}$ T |
| | | | $\dfrac{\text{-}}{\text{nearby}}$ T |
| | | | $\dfrac{\text{-et}}{\text{equality}}$ T |
| | | | $\dfrac{\text{slave}}{\text{slavery}}$ T |
| | | | $\dfrac{\text{in-}}{\text{infection}}$ T |
| | | | $\dfrac{\text{me-sur-ing}}{\text{measuring}}$ T |

**Instructional Implications**

Child 3 averaged three Tolds on each running record. Again, too many. The majority of the Tolds occurred on words that were content-specific vocabulary. This signals the need to provide a richer book introduction to build understanding around unfamiliar vocabulary. If there are too many unfamiliar words, a different text may be more suitable for this child.

# CHAPTER 9

# Addressing High-Frequency Words

I t is frustrating when we see children make errors on words we have taught them. We may be in for a big surprise, however, if we assume that just because we taught something the children learned it. There is often a big difference in the words we *think* children know and those they *actually* know. Analyzing running records helps us check assumptions by revealing the high-frequency words children can identify and read automatically—and those they can't.

## FROM PRACTICE TO PROFICIENCY

The chart on the following pages captures a child's reading of *The Ant and the Grasshopper* by Kelly Moodie (Level H, running words: 194). Use the information to score, analyze, and calculate the accuracy and SC rates. (See answer key at the end of the chapter.) When you are finished, write your thoughts about the child in the space at the end of the chart, using the following questions to guide your thinking.

- Did anything surprise me?
- Is there a pattern to the types of words the child missed?
- Is there a pattern to the sources of information the child used or neglected?
- What do I notice about the self-corrections?

| Text | Running Record | Count | | Information Used | |
|---|---|---|---|---|---|
| | | E | SC | E<br>M S V | SC<br>M S V |

It was a long, hot summer.
Grasshopper was happy.

He sang all day long.
He slept in the sun.
He loved being lazy!

✓ ✓ ✓ ✓ ✓ ✓

✓ $\frac{is}{was}$ ✓

✓ ✓ $\frac{a}{all}$ ✓ ✓

✓ ✓ ✓ ✓ ✓

$\frac{It}{He}$ | SC ✓ ✓ ✓

Ant had no time to sing or snooze.

She worked hard all day long
looking for food to eat.
She loved being busy!

✓ ✓ ✓ ✓ ✓ ✓ $\frac{and}{or}$ ✓

✓ ✓ ✓ ✓ ✓ ✓

✓ ✓ ✓ ✓ $\frac{get}{eat}$

✓ ✓ ✓ ✓

"Relax! Don't work so hard,"
said Grasshopper with a smile.

"Summer is the time to have fun,"
he said.

✓ ✓ ✓ $\frac{too}{so}$ ✓

✓ ✓ ✓ ✓ ✓

✓ ✓ ✓ ✓ ✓ ✓

✓ ✓

| Text | Running Record | Count | | Information Used | |
|---|---|---|---|---|---|
| | | E | SC | E M S V | SC M S V |

"It will be winter soon," said Ant. "I need to make a warm home. I need to gather food."

"What will you do when winter comes?" she asked Grasshopper.

✓ $\frac{would}{will}$ ✓ ✓ ✓ ✓

✓ ✓ ✓ ✓ ✓ ✓

✓ ✓ ✓ ✓ ✓

$\frac{Where}{What} \Big| When$ ✓ ✓ ✓ ✓ ✓

✓ ✓ ✓

"Winter is far away," said Grasshopper.

✓ ✓ ✓ ✓

✓ ✓

He went on singing. Ant went on working.

✓ $\frac{goes}{went}$ ✓ ✓

✓ $\frac{goes}{went} \Big| SC$ ✓ ✓

| Text | Running Record | Count | | Information Used | |
|---|---|---|---|---|---|
| | | E | SC | E<br>M S V | SC<br>M S V |

Summer lasted a long time,
just as Grasshopper said.

But winter finally came,
just as Ant said.

✓ ✓ ✓ ✓ ✓

✓ like ✓ ✓
   as

✓ ✓ ✓ ✓

✓ like | SC ✓ ✓
   as |

During the winter,
grasshopper was very cold.
He was very hungry, too.
He asked Ant for help.

✓ ✓ ✓

✓ ✓ ✓ ✓

✓ ✓ ✓ ✓ ✓

✓ ✓ ✓ ✓ ✓

Ant frowned.
"You sang all summer long.
You slept in the sun.
I will give you food and a
warm place to stay.
But next summer you must
work, too," she said.

✓ ✓

✓ ✓ ✓ ✓ ✓

✓ ✓ on | SC ✓ ✓ R
    in |

✓ ✓ get ✓ ✓ ✓ ✓
    give

✓ ✓ ✓ ✓

✓ ✓ ✓ ✓ ✓

✓ ✓ ✓ ✓

| Text | Running Record | Count | | Information Used | |
|---|---|---|---|---|---|
| | | E | SC | E M S V | SC M S V |

When summer came again,
Ant worked very hard.
So did Grasshopper.
Hop! Hop! Hop!
Grasshopper had finally learned
his lesson.

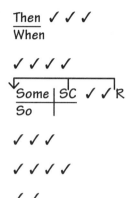

Then ✓ ✓ ✓
─────
When

✓ ✓ ✓ ✓

Some | SC ✓ ✓ R
─────
So

✓ ✓ ✓

✓ ✓ ✓ ✓

✓ ✓

## Guiding Questions

- Did anything surprise me?
- Is there a pattern to the types of words the child missed?
- Is there a pattern to the sources of information the child used or neglected?
- What do I notice about the self-corrections?

## Your Thoughts

## Our Thoughts

The text was read with 94% accuracy and a self-correction rate of 1:4, but there is much more to learn about the child's reading. An examination of the errors reveals a pattern in which the child maintained meaning and structure and at times attended to some visual information. Moving beyond this analysis and looking more closely at the types of words read incorrectly, we find they are all high-frequency words that should have been read accurately at this level. When the child does self-correct, the self-correction involves known words. Further, most words that are self-corrected appear more than once on the page, giving the child a second opportunity to detect the error and fix it. There are also two examples (*some/so* and *on/in*) where the initial attempt fits meaning and structure, but when the child continues reading, he realizes that meaning was not maintained after the point of error, triggering him to reread and self-correct.

# TYPES OF WORDS CHILDREN SHOULD KNOW

High-frequency words are words that appear repeatedly in and across texts. There have been lots of high-frequency word lists over the years. Some such as the Dolch List (1936), contain the most frequently occurring words within a specific publisher's text set, such as a basal reader. Others are more generic and contain commonly used words in a variety of text types, from Scripture to a favorite novel.

Edward Fry (1999) created a list for which, he claimed, the first 25 words comprise a third of all words that appear in printed material and the first 100 words comprise half of all words that appear in printed material.

There are two types of high-frequency words that appear on high-frequency word lists. The first are regular high-frequency words, such as *but, can, did, get, go, him, not,* and *up.* The second are irregular words such as *is, of, said, the, two,* and *was.* Because children will encounter these words over and over, they must learn to recognize them automatically.

Jan created a list of high-frequency words grouped by text levels A–I (Richardson, 2016). She reviewed leveled books from a variety of publishers and identified 10 words that frequently appear at each level. She considered the ease at which the words could be learned. See the list below.

| Sight Word Chart for Monitoring Progress | | | | | | | |
|---|---|---|---|---|---|---|---|
| Level A | Level B | Level C | Level D | Level E | Level F | Levels G–I Set I | Levels G–I Set 2 (more challenging) |
| am | dad | and | day | all | came | didn't | again |
| at | he | are | down | away | have | don't | because |
| can | in | come | into | back | help | eat | could |
| go | it | for | looking | big | next | from | does |
| is | look | got | she | her | now | give | every |
| like | mom | here | they | over | one | good | laugh |
| me | my | not | went | this | some | make | many |
| see | on | play | where | want | then | of | new |
| the | up | said | will | who | was | out | night |
| to | we | you | your | with | what | saw | very |
| | | | | | | were | walk |
| | | | | | | when | why |

High-utility words are words that appear in books specifically for reading instruction or in their everyday environments. They have high value and are familiar to most beginning readers. They fit into one of three groups: personal, school, and publisher-specific.

## High-Utility Words

| Type | Definition | Example |
|---|---|---|
| **Personal** | Words that are personal and have meaning to an individual child | child's name, names of siblings, names of pets, favorites (superhero – *Batman*, food – *pizza*, game – *Minecraft*, team name – *Tigers*) |
| **School** | Words displayed in the classroom or on school property or words associated with school | labels (e.g.,clock, desk, pencil sharpener), art room, bus, school name, colors and numbers, days of the week, months, direction words (e.g., *write, draw, circle*), teachers' names, classmates' names |
| **Publisher-Specific** | Words commonly used by publishers in material for reading instruction. The words may not be found on lists such as Fry's. | *asked, asleep, along, beautiful, clever, help, hungry, play, please, shouted, sorry, thank you* |

While many high-frequency words and high-utility words are decodable, children should develop a visual memory of them so they can read them quickly and accurately.

The words children need to know with automaticity change over time, based on their growing competencies and the types of texts they are reading. For example, in early-level texts, words such as *the*, *can*, and *to* are considered high-frequency words. More complex texts contain not only those words, which children need to have well under control, but also new, more sophisticated words that occur frequently. For example, words such as *could*, *would*, and *does*, and contractions that contain those words, will begin to appear. Similarly, children will encounter lots of words that begin with *wh* and *th*. Children who have not mastered *the* are likely to be confused when *they*, *their*, *there*, and *they're* appear, which can cause them to shift their focus to the word and letter level. When that happens, children get fixated on the visual information without integrating meaning, which can lead them to revert to a letter-by-letter sound analysis of known and irregular high-frequency words such as *said*.

# KNOWN WORDS SUPPORT READERS AND WRITERS

Automatically recognizing a large number of high-frequency words and high-utility words supports children's successful reading. Automaticity supports early reading behaviors such as one-to-one correspondence as children monitor the number of words on a page and begin to connect what they say to what appears in print. Also, early readers use high-frequency words as visual anchors in text and as gateways to learning more about the visual aspects of print.

Once children have a bank of known words, they can use parts of those words to problem-solve unknown words. For example, if a child encounters the unknown word *sandy*, he may be able to use his knowledge of *and* to figure out *sandy*. Known words that contain units or patterns, such as consonant blends and digraphs, *r*-controlled vowels, and other vowel combinations, support children in decoding words that contain those same patterns. At first, those known units or patterns help readers solve unknown one-syllable words by breaking the word at the onset and rime (e.g., *b all*, *sh ark*, *bl ock*), but eventually the process of using known words or word parts can help children solve more complex multisyllabic words. Using salient units in known words becomes part of a child's repertoire of decoding strategies and enables their flexible use of visual information.

For children to use parts of words and patterns in words, they must know words that contain those parts and patterns. Clay (2016) provides a definition of what it means to know a word. She defines a known word as a word the child can read and write quickly, without lapses and regardless of context.

To explain further the journey a word takes to becoming known, Clay developed a scale that begins when a word is new to a child and progresses to when it is known. Along the way, children will know the word in one context but may be easily confused when seeing the same word in a different context (e.g., the word appears in a tricky or unusual language structure, the word begins with a lowercase letter vs. the same word beginning with an uppercase letter: Come *here* vs. *Here* you are). After repeated exposure to words in continuous text, along with practicing those words in isolation, the child comes to know them, regardless of where or how they appear. At that point, the child can use the units and patterns those words contain to solve unfamiliar but similar words.

Furthermore, automatically recognizing words in a text contributes to phrased and fluent reading. It reduces a child's cognitive load, freeing the child to think about the story and attend to the visual information within the word. Known words, and the ways in which they sustain fluent reading, support a child's ability to construct and maintain meaning.

### *Teaching Students High-Frequency Words*

Moving a word from new to known can occur in a variety of settings. In this section, we discuss the instructional implications for helping children build a bank of known words.

### Individual Instruction

- Teach the child how to learn words by tapping into his visual memory. Follow these steps:

    1    Have the child locate a word in a text and frame it with his index fingers.

    2    Have the child say the word slowly while sliding his finger left to right under the word.

    3    Have the child look at the word again.

    4    Have the child close his eyes and visualize the word.

    5    Have the child write the word and check it against the word in the text.

    6    Have the child reread the sentence from the text that contains the word.

    7    Have the child write the word several more times on different surfaces, using a variety of tools and mediums.

- Choose a word from a text that the child has read and have her construct it with magnetic letters. Once the child has constructed the word, ask her to mix up the letters and reconstruct it. Ask her to reread the sentence from the text that contains the word. Repeat the procedure several times on different words, asking the child to check her work each time.

- Select a book that contains a new word and have the child locate it and frame it with his index fingers before reading. After the reading, use a masking card to frame the word and have the child read it quickly.

- Write some words that begin with *th* and *wh* on 3-x-5 index cards. Often, when children come to a word that begins with one of those consonant digraphs, they call out any word that begins with them (e.g., the word is *this* and the child says *that*, *there*…). With a blank 3-x-5 card, cover the word except for the initial digraph. Before the child attempts to read the word, have her stop and watch as you reveal the rest of it. This prevents the child from using only visual information at the beginning of the word and guessing at the word. Reading is not guessing! Move onto the next word and repeat the procedure. Over time, children recognize these words automatically and are no longer confused by words that are visually similar and may have similar meanings (e.g., *that* for *this*; *these* for *those*).

### Small-Group Instruction

After reading a book, choose a high-frequency word that is new to students and have them locate, frame, and read it. Select from the following multisensory activities to help them learn the word automatically by attending to the detailed visual information. (For more information, see *The Next Step Forward in Guided Reading*, 2016).

### *Mix and Fix*

- Write the word on a dry-erase board.

- Ask students to look at each letter as you slide an index card across the word, from left to right.

- Give students the letters to make the word. Keep the word on the dry-erase board in case students need a reference.

- After students make the word, have them say it as they slide their finger under it to check their accuracy. This supports orthographic mapping.

- Have students mix up the letters and remake the word, from left to right.

### Trace the Word

- Ask students to trace the magnetic letters for the word or write the word on an index card.

- Have them say the word slowly as they trace or write it. By doing so, they link the visual and phonological information.

- Ask them to check the word with their finger while they say it naturally.

- Have them quickly read the word once more.

### Write and Retrieve

- Have students write the new word on a dry-erase board as they say it naturally. Check their work and ask them to erase it.

- Dictate a known word for students to write. Check and erase.

- Dictate the new high-frequency word again for them to retrieve from memory and rewrite.

### Other Activities to Build a Bank of Known Words

- Establish fluency by having students write the word many times within a set time frame (e.g., 15 seconds) on different surfaces such as Boogie Boards, chalkboards, Magic Slates, and dry-erase boards.

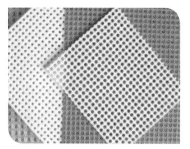

- Give each child a small piece of screen or needlepoint plastic. Have the children place it on the table with a piece of white paper on top. Then have the children carefully write the word using a crayon, pressing forcefully. This will create a bumpy surface and allow for a multisensory version of the word that they can trace with their finger. Once the children finish, have them select a new color and repeat the process.

- Have them review the word over several days to bring it to automaticity.

## Whole-Group Instruction

- Ask students to locate and frame high-frequency words during shared reading and interactive or shared writing. While one child is framing a word in a text (e.g., a big book, a digital text, a collaborative piece of writing), the rest of the children can practice writing the word on individual dry-erase boards or chalkboards. Vary the children that come to the chart to differentiate and reinforce words on which individual children are working.

- Have children practice writing high-frequency words at their seats using shaving cream. Ideally, give each child an individualized list of words to practice.

## Independent Practice

- Have the students practice writing known words sequentially and cumulatively, as shown in the example at right. Have the children start by writing the first letter of the word on the first line, the first two letters on the second line, and so forth until they complete the word.

w

we

wen

went

- Create a Concentration-style game by writing high-frequency words on separate index cards, two cards for each word. Put children in groups of two to four. Shuffle the cards and place them face down. Have children take turns turning over two cards, trying to find two words that match. If the cards match, the child picks up the cards and places them in his or her pile. If the two cards do not match, the child turns them over, and it is the next child's turn to pick two cards. When all of the cards are matched, have children read their words and count the matches they made.

- For each child, select words for independent practice. Then, in the first column of the reproducible form, "Trace It, Write It, Don't Look at It," write the words. Give the form to the child and have her trace the word in the first column with a colored pencil and then write the word in the second column with a different colored pencil. Then have her fold back the third column, so the examples are hidden, and write the word independently without looking. When she is finished, ask her to unfold the paper and check her work. Repeat with the next word on the list.

*Appendix C, page 238, and scholastic.com/ ResourcesNSFRR*

# CLOSING THOUGHT

Analyzing running records for missed and self-corrected high-frequency words is important because it helps you decide which words students need to practice. Also, voluminous reading and writing exposes children to high-frequency words and helps them see those words in meaningful connected text.

Until words are automatic, children may make errors, such as reading *this* for *that*, and ignore the errors because the words look similar and have virtually the same meaning. Eventually, the child needs to shift from making and not recognizing errors to monitoring for errors and self-correcting. Only then will they become automatic and accurate readers. Analyzing running records over time can reveal this progression. Be sure to document the increase in the number and types of words a child knows. There are a number of ways to do that, for example, using Jan's Sight Word Checklists in her book *The Next Step Forward in Word Study and Phonics* (2019). When you couple that information with running record analysis, you can monitor students' progress and make informed instructional decisions.

**Answer key for the practice activity on pages 154–158:**

| Text | Running Record | Count E | Count SC | Information Used E M S V | Information Used SC M S V |
|------|----------------|---------|----------|-------------------------|---------------------------|
| It was a long, hot summer. Grasshopper was happy. He sang all day long. He slept in the sun. He loved being lazy! | ✓ ✓ ✓ ✓ ✓ ✓ | | | | |
| | ✓ is/was ✓ | 1 | | Ⓜ Ⓢ Ⓥ | |
| | ✓ ✓ a/all ✓ ✓ | 1 | | Ⓜ Ⓢ Ⓥ | |
| | ✓ ✓ ✓ ✓ ✓ | | | | |
| | It\|SC He\| ✓ ✓ ✓ | | 1 | Ⓜ Ⓢ V | M S Ⓥ |
| Ant had no time to sing or snooze. She worked hard all day long looking for food to eat. She loved being busy! | ✓ ✓ ✓ ✓ ✓ ✓ and/or ✓ | 1 | | Ⓜ Ⓢ V | |
| | ✓ ✓ ✓ ✓ ✓ ✓ | | | | |
| | ✓ ✓ ✓ ✓ get/eat | 1 | | Ⓜ Ⓢ Ⓥ | |
| | ✓ ✓ ✓ ✓ | | | | |

| Text | Running Record | Count | | Information Used | |
|------|----------------|-------|------|------------------|------|
| | | E | SC | E<br>M S V | SC<br>M S V |
| <br>"Relax! Don't work so hard," said Grasshopper with a smile.<br><br>"Summer is the time to have fun," he said.<br><br>7 | ✓ ✓ ✓ too ✓<br>      so<br><br>✓ ✓ ✓ ✓ ✓<br><br>✓ ✓ ✓ ✓ ✓ ✓<br><br>✓ ✓ | 1 | | (M)(S)(V) | |
| "It will be winter soon," said Ant.<br>"I need to make a warm home.<br>I need to gather food."<br><br>"What will you do when winter comes?" she asked Grasshopper.<br><br><br>8 | ✓ would ✓ ✓ ✓ ✓<br>   will<br><br>✓ ✓ ✓ ✓ ✓ ✓<br><br>✓ ✓ ✓ ✓ ✓<br><br>Where \| When ✓✓✓✓✓✓<br>What   \|<br><br>✓ ✓ ✓ | 1<br><br><br><br><br>1 | | (M)(S)(V)<br><br><br><br><br>(M)(S)(V) | |
| <br>"Winter is far away," said Grasshopper.<br><br>10 | ✓ ✓ ✓ ✓<br><br>✓ ✓ | | | | |

| Text | Running Record | Count | | Information Used | |
|---|---|:---:|:---:|:---:|:---:|
| | | **E** | **SC** | **E**<br>**M S V** | **SC**<br>**M S V** |
| <br>He went on singing.<br>Ant went on working.<br>11 | ✓ goes ✓ ✓<br>   ‾went‾ | 1 | | Ⓜ Ⓢ V | |
| | ✓ goes │ SC ✓ ✓<br>   ‾went‾ │ | | 1 | Ⓜ Ⓢ V | M S Ⓥ |
| Summer lasted a long time,<br>just as Grasshopper said.<br><br>But winter finally came,<br>just as Ant said.<br> | ✓ ✓ ✓ ✓<br>✓ like ✓ ✓<br>   ‾as‾ | 1 | | Ⓜ Ⓢ V | |
| | ✓ ✓ ✓ ✓<br>✓ like │ SC ✓ ✓<br>   ‾as‾ │ | | 1 | Ⓜ Ⓢ V | M S Ⓥ |
| During the winter,<br>grasshopper was very cold.<br>He was very hungry, too.<br>He asked Ant for help.<br> | ✓ ✓ ✓<br>✓ ✓ ✓ ✓<br>✓ ✓ ✓ ✓ ✓<br>✓ ✓ ✓ ✓ ✓ | | | | |

| Text | Running Record | Count | | Information Used | |
|---|---|---|---|---|---|
| | | E | SC | E M S V | SC M S V |
| <br>Ant frowned.<br>"You sang all summer long.<br>You slept in the sun.<br>I will give you food and a<br>warm place to stay.<br>But next summer you must<br>work, too," she said. | ✓ ✓ | | | | |
| | ✓ ✓ ✓ ✓ ✓ | | | | |
| | ✓ ✓ on\|SC ✓✓R <br> in\| | | 1 | Ⓜ ⓈⓋ | M S Ⓥ |
| | ✓ ✓ get ✓ ✓ ✓ ✓ <br> give | 1 | | Ⓜ ⓈⓋ | |
| | ✓ ✓ ✓ ✓ | | | | |
| | ✓ ✓ ✓ ✓ ✓ | | | | |
| | ✓ ✓ ✓ ✓ | | | | |
| <br>When summer came again,<br>Ant worked very hard.<br>So did Grasshopper.<br>Hop! Hop! Hop!<br>Grasshopper had finally learned<br>his lesson. | Then ✓ ✓ ✓ <br> When | 1 | | Ⓜ ⓈⓋ | |
| | ✓ ✓ ✓ ✓ | | | | |
| | Some\|SC ✓ ✓R <br> So\| | | 1 | Ⓜ ⓈⓋ | M S Ⓥ |
| | ✓ ✓ ✓ | | | | |
| | ✓ ✓ ✓ ✓ | | | | |
| | ✓ ✓ | | | | |

# CHAPTER 10

# Supporting Children's Use of Visual Information

In this chapter, we discuss children's use of visual information—the ways in which children draw upon the alphabetic principle, or the connection between letters and sounds. Children's use of visual information should not be analyzed in isolation. Rather, it should be analyzed in light of their understandings of the text, knowledge of the world, vocabulary, and language use. It should be situated within the complex task of constructing meaning from continuous text. We capture that process on a running record as we observe and code how a child works on text, gaining insight into the processing system that children are bringing under control. Analyzing running records for patterns in the ways children use or neglect visual information can guide our next steps when making decisions and planning instruction.

**Beginning Letters**
- single consonants (m-om)/initial vowels (*i-t*)

**Digraphs**
- *ch-, th-, sh-, wh-*

**Consonant Blends/Clusters**
- *cr-, st-, pl-*

**Letter by Letter**
- CVC words (*h-o-t*)

**Endings**
- *-ing, -s, -es, -ed, -ly*

**Efficient Units and Patterns**
- short-vowel patterns (*-at, -et, -in, -ot, -ut*)
- long-vowel patterns (*-ay, -ee, -igh, -oa, -y*)
- *r*-controlled vowels (*-ar, -er, -ir, -or, -ur*)
- dipthongs (*-oi, -oy, -ou, -ow*)

**Multisyllabic Words**
- two-syllable words (*bed-room*)
- three-syllable words (*grass-hop-per*)

# FROM PRACTICE TO PROFICIENCY

The chart below captures a child's reading of *Bird's New Nest* by Tammi J. Salzano (Level F, running words: 213). Use the information in it to score, analyze, and calculate the accuracy and SC rates. (See the answer key at the end of the chapter.) When you are finished, write your thoughts about the child in the space at the end of the chart, using the following questions to guide your thinking.

- Did anything surprise me?
- Do I notice a pattern in the way the child uses or neglects visual information?
- What letters and letter combinations or units does the child use when decoding?
- What examples show the child's flexible use of visual information?

| Text | Running Record | Count | | Information Used | |
|---|---|---|---|---|---|
| | | **E** | **SC** | **E**<br>**M S V** | **SC**<br>**M S V** |
| Bird needs a new home.<br>She will build a nest!<br>What can Bird use to make the nest? | ✓ n-ee-d\| ✓ ✓ ✓<br>— needs \|<br><br>✓ ✓ b-✓ ✓ n-e-st\| ✓<br>— build — nest \|<br><br>Wh-at\|w-hat\|A\| ✓✓ us ✓✓✓✓<br>What \| \|T — use | | | | |
| Bird finds some sticks in the garden.<br>She can make her nest with sticks! | ✓ f-in-d-s \|SC ✓ ✓ ✓ ✓ g-ar-✓<br>— finds \| — garden<br><br>✓ ✓ ✓ ✓ ✓ ✓ ✓ | | | | |

| Text | Running Record | Count | | Information Used | |
|---|---|---|---|---|---|
| | | **E** | **SC** | **E**<br>**M S V** | **SC**<br>**M S V** |

Bird sits on the sticks.
Does Bird like the sticks?
No. The sticks are too sharp.

✓ ✓ ✓ ✓ ✓

$\dfrac{\text{Do-s}}{\text{Does}}$ ✓ ✓ ✓ ✓

✓ ✓ ✓ ✓ ✓ $\dfrac{\text{sh-ar-p}✓}{\text{sharp}}$

Bird finds some hay.
She can make her nest with hay!

✓ ✓ ✓ $\dfrac{\text{h-}✓}{\text{hay}}$

✓ ✓ ✓ ✓ ✓ ✓ ✓

Bird sits on the hay.
Does Bird like the hay?
No. The hay is too itchy.

✓ ✓ ✓ ✓ ✓

$\dfrac{\text{Do-s}}{\text{Does}}$ | SC ✓ ✓ ✓

✓ ✓ ✓ ✓ ✓ $\dfrac{\text{it-ch}}{\text{itchy}}$ | itch

Bird finds some mud.
She can make her nest with mud!

✓ ✓ ✓ ✓

✓ ✓ ✓ ✓ ✓ ✓ ✓

| Text | Running Record | Count | | Information Used | |
|---|---|---|---|---|---|
| | | E | SC | E<br>M S V | SC<br>M S V |
| <br><br>Bird sits in the mud.<br>Does Bird like the mud?<br>No. The mud is too messy. | ✓ ✓ ✓ ✓<br><br>$\dfrac{\text{Did}}{\text{Does}}$ ✓ ✓ ✓ ✓<br><br>✓ ✓ ✓ ✓ ✓ $\dfrac{\text{muddy}}{\text{messy}}$ | | | | |
| <br><br>Bird finds some flowers.<br>She can make her nest with flowers! | ✓ ✓ ✓ ✓<br><br>✓ ✓ ✓ ✓ ✓ ✓ | | | | |
| <br><br>Bird sits on the flowers.<br>Does Bird like the flowers?<br>No. The flowers are too big. | ✓ ✓ ✓ ✓<br><br>$\dfrac{\text{Did}}{\text{Does}}$ ✓ ✓ ✓ ✓<br><br>✓ ✓ ✓ ✓ ✓ | | | | |
| <br><br>Bird finds some rocks.<br>She can make her nest with rocks! | ✓ ✓ ✓ ✓<br><br>✓ ✓ ✓ ✓ ✓ ✓ | | | | |

| Text | Running Record | Count | | Information Used | |
|---|---|---|---|---|---|
| | | **E** | **SC** | **E**<br>**M S V** | **SC**<br>**M S V** |

Bird sits on the rocks.
Does Bird like the rocks?
No. The rocks are too bumpy.

✓ ✓ ✓ ✓ ✓

✓ ✓ ✓ ✓ ✓

✓ ✓ ✓ ✓ ✓ jump | bump | bumping | SC
⎯⎯⎯
bumpy |

Bird is sad.
What can she use to make
her nest?
She will go under the tree.
She will think about what to do.

✓ ✓ mad
⎯⎯
sad

✓ ✓ ✓ have ✓ ✓
⎯⎯
use

✓ ✓

✓ ✓ ✓ ✓ ✓ ✓

✓ ✓ th-in-k ✓ a-b-out | aboot | SC ✓ ✓
⎯⎯⎯⎯ ⎯⎯⎯⎯
think about |

Wait! What is that under the tree?
Bird sees grass under the tree.

✓ ✓ ✓ this ✓ ✓ ✓
⎯⎯
that

✓ ✓ ✓ ✓ ✓ ✓

Bird sits on the grass.
Does Bird like the grass?
Yes! The grass is soft.
Bird can make her nest with grass!

✓ ✓ ✓ ✓ ✓

✓ ✓ ✓ ✓ ✓

✓ ✓ ✓ ✓ ✓

✓ ✓ ✓ ✓ ✓ ✓

| Text | Running Record | Count | | Information Used | |
|------|----------------|-------|---|------------------|---|
| | | E | SC | E<br>M S V | SC<br>M S V |

✓ ✓ ✓ ✓

✓ <u>likes</u> ✓ ✓ ✓
   loves

The child read word by word at the beginning. As the story progressed, he read in phrases and was very fast.

## Your Thoughts

### Guiding Questions

- Did anything surprise me?
- Do I notice a pattern in the way the child uses or neglects visual information?
- What letters and letter combinations or units does the child use when decoding?
- What examples show the child's flexible use of visual information?

## Our Thoughts

It is surprising in this running record that the child didn't reread. His attempts show he is making sense of the text, but it may only be at the page or sentence level. He demonstrates flexibility in many places (e.g., *jump/bumpy; bump; bumping; SC*), and even though it yields a self-correction, rereading would have supported the work he did. The child also relies on the predictable pattern for support, which is problematic because he uses the repetition to carry him and does not initiate the visual analysis needed (e.g., *did/does*). The recording clearly demonstrates that the child uses many units quickly and efficiently (e.g., digraphs, blends, vowel combinations, and *r*-controlled vowels) and he also solves by analogy (e.g., *jump* to *bump*). Finally, as the child's reading rate increases, he fails to monitor or engage in more detailed visual analysis on words that make sense and have some visual similarity at the beginning and end.

# HOW CHILDREN USE VISUAL INFORMATION

As children learn to attend to print and understand letter-sound relationships, they come to expect visual information to assist them. Visual information allows children to engage in strategic behaviors such as monitoring (see Chapter 7), cross-checking, and integrated attempts.

## Cross-Checking

Cross-checking occurs when children use one information source, such as visual, to confirm or check another information source, such as meaning or structure. You can find evidence of cross-checking by analyzing errors and self-corrections on running records and gain information about the child's use of visual information. If a child said *stones* instead of *rocks* when reading *Bird's New Nest*, we would infer that he used meaning and structure in the initial attempt. If the child self-corrected, we would conclude he used some visual information to cross-check and self-correct (see Example 1).

If a child said *red* for *rocks*, we would infer that he relied only on visual information. If he self-corrected, we would conclude he used meaning to cross-check and self-correct (see Example 2). If the child engages in a sequential search of the visual information, we would likely hear in the child's voice his letter/sound analysis. This would be coded on the running record as r-o-ck-s and would be considered a self-correction using additional visual information.

**Example 1**

| Text | Running Record | Count | | Information Used | |
|---|---|---|---|---|---|
| | | E | SC | E<br>M S V | SC<br>M S V |
| Bird sits on the rocks.<br>Does Bird like the rocks?<br>No. The rocks are too bumpy. | ✓ ✓ ✓ ✓ stones \| SC<br>———— rocks \|<br>✓ ✓ ✓ ✓ ✓<br>✓ ✓ ✓ ✓ ✓ ✓ | | 1 | Ⓜ Ⓢ V | M S Ⓥ |

**Example 2**

| Text | Running Record | Count | | Information Used | |
|------|---------------|-------|------|-----------------|------|
| | | E | SC | E<br>M S V | SC<br>M S V |
| Bird sits on the rocks.<br>Does Bird like the rocks?<br>No. The rocks are too bumpy.<br>12 | ✓ ✓ ✓ ✓ red \|SC<br>──────<br>rocks\|<br><br>✓ ✓ ✓ ✓<br><br>✓ ✓ ✓ ✓ ✓ | | 1 | M S Ⓥ | Ⓜ Ⓢ V |

On the running record, cross-checking is most apparent when the child attempts the word twice. The first attempt will clearly show the child's use of one source of information. The second attempt will show how he or she used another source of information to check the first one. In the examples we have provided, the second attempt led to a self-correction, but that is not always the case. For example, if a child's first attempt is *sister* for *mother*, we would circle meaning and structure. If the child's second attempt was *mom* for *mother*, we could further infer the child had cross-checked with some visual information, even though it did not result in a self-correction.

## Integrated Attempts

As a child becomes more proficient, her cross-checking becomes more sophisticated, and she will begin to use multiple information sources on initial reading attempts. When she is decoding a word, for example, we may see evidence of her using an initial letter, blend, or digraph in combination with meaning and structure. For beginning readers, this may produce an integrated error such as *home* for *house*. But as her use of visual information evolves and becomes more sophisticated, she is likely to pay attention to additional details, such as endings, vowel combinations, phonograms, and orthographic patterns. When the child reads *home* for *house*, she may recognize that there is no /m/ in *house* or may notice the /ou/ and connect the unit to a known word, such as *out*. Visual analysis happens rapidly and, unless the child tells you what she notices (e.g., "There's no *m*!") or emphasizes a sound with her voice (*h-ou-se*), we can only infer the child has engaged in further searching. It is critical to record as accurately as possible the way the child decodes or takes a word apart. Doing that will provide insight into the types of visual information the reader is using.

Even though children make integrated attempts, using all sources of information simultaneously, they may revert to a nonproductive letter-by-letter reading when confronted with an unknown and unfamiliar word. When that happens, consider the cognitive load the task and text are placing on the child. As teachers, we must determine why this is happening and figure out how to teach in a way that supports the child's use of meaning and efficient decoding skills. Sometimes it has to do with how well the child knows a letter combination or unit. For example, a child may solve the word *eat* but not the word *peach*. They know /ea/ as a unit in *eat*, but when it appears embedded in *peach*, the child reverts to letter-by-letter analysis of the word: /p//e//a//ch/. In this example, the child does not recognize /ea/ as a unit in the word *peach* and, therefore, defaults to an unproductive decoding strategy. Knowing /ea/ as a unit will get the child closer to reading *peach*, but if the word is not in her vocabulary, it will not activate meaning and the child will be unable to confirm if the response is correct.

The running record at the start of this chapter that begins on page 173 provides evidence of the types of visual information the child has used and neglected. Return to that record to see how he successfully used the following units and how they were recorded: /ee/, /st/, /ar/, /sh/, /it/, /ch/, /ump/, /th/, and /out/. The record also reveals that the child needs to develop flexibility with vowels. For example, if he tries a short-vowel sound that doesn't make sense (*us*), he needs to learn to switch to a long-vowel sound (*use*). He also needs practice with other long-vowel sounds (*-y* as long *e* in *itchy* and *bumpy*), as well as with irregular high-frequency words which need to be automatically recognized such as *what* and *does*. (For more on high-frequency words as a source of visual information, see Chapter 9.)

## HOW CHILDREN MAKE DECISIONS USING VISUAL INFORMATION

Sometimes it's helpful to take a close look at children's integrated attempts as a series of decisions. After the child makes a first attempt, he may then confirm the response by checking the visual information sequentially. If he is satisfied, he continues reading. However, if he isn't, he ideally initiates a more detailed visual search or draws on other sources of information. The chart on the next page highlights possible responses and decisions, which show the complexity of a child's process. The systematic observation and recording of a child's reading work, including error and self-correction behavior, allow us to infer children's decisions during their reading of continuous text.

**Using Visual Information**

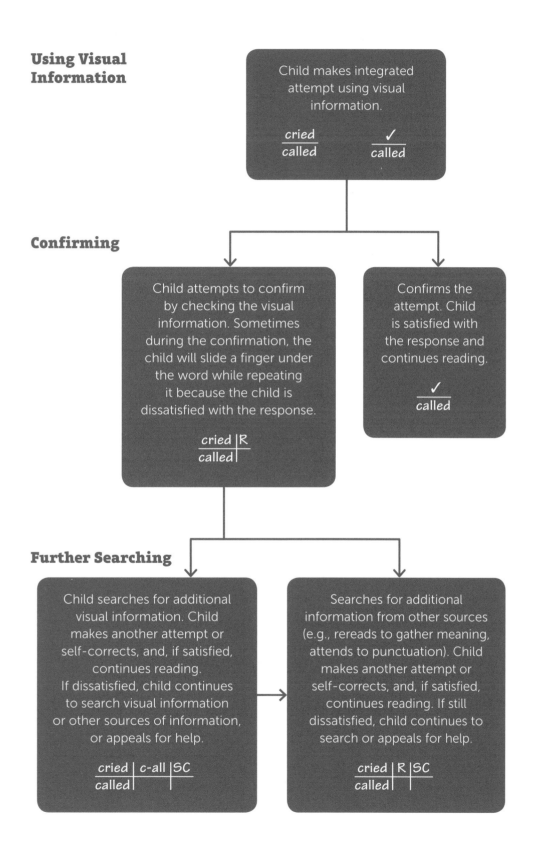

Child makes integrated attempt using visual information.

$$\frac{cried}{called} \qquad \frac{\checkmark}{called}$$

**Confirming**

Child attempts to confirm by checking the visual information. Sometimes during the confirmation, the child will slide a finger under the word while repeating it because the child is dissatisfied with the response.

$$\frac{cried}{called}\Big|^R$$

Confirms the attempt. Child is satisfied with the response and continues reading.

$$\frac{\checkmark}{called}$$

**Further Searching**

Child searches for additional visual information. Child makes another attempt or self-corrects, and, if satisfied, continues reading.
If dissatisfied, child continues to search visual information or other sources of information, or appeals for help.

$$\frac{cried}{called}\Big|\, c\text{-}all \,\Big|\, SC$$

Searches for additional information from other sources (e.g., rereads to gather meaning, attends to punctuation). Child makes another attempt or self-corrects, and, if satisfied, continues reading. If still dissatisfied, child continues to search or appeals for help.

$$\frac{cried}{called}\Big|\, R \,\Big|\, SC$$

## Teaching Students to Use Visual Information

Attending to visual information and teaching children how to use it when reading should permeate instruction. In this section, we will discuss some instructional implications for using visual information while maintaining meaning.

### Individual Instruction

- When a child comes to a word and responds with a substitution that makes sense, such as *duck* for *goose*, first wait to see if she monitors to notice the visual inconsistency. If she doesn't, when she completes the sentence or page, say, "Something doesn't look right, can you find it?" This gives the child the opportunity to notice the error. If the child doesn't notice, say, "What letter would you expect to see at the beginning of duck?", which should prompt the child to check the initial visual information and recognize the error. If she is unable to use the /g/ to read *goose*, ask her to reread the sentence and produce the initial sound when she comes to *goose*. Finally, have the child check the word *goose* by sliding her finger under it while saying it slowly to confirm that the sounds she hears match the letters she sees.

- Help children develop a known-word vocabulary that contains words with generative parts and will therefore assist with visual analysis. For example, if a child knows the word *car*, the *r*-controlled vowel pattern can assist him in solving *shark*. To develop a known-word vocabulary, highlight these types of words in text using a masking card and have the child read them quickly. He can also write the words using a variety of tools (markers, water pens, chalk) and surfaces (dry-erase, chalkboard, paper). Remember, a child truly knows a word when he can read it, write it, and use it to solve similar words (see Chapter 9).

- To teach left-to-right analysis of words, choose a target word and slide a card across it as the child reads, stopping briefly to isolate and show the efficient units of visual information. This is especially helpful for children who are only using the initial visual information because it shows them how to visually search across a word.

### Small-Group Instruction

- During a book introduction, when introducing the names of characters or unfamiliar vocabulary, don't just have children repeat the words, expecting they'll remember them. Instead, have children combine meaning-making and visual information in the words. For example, if you're introducing a text about porcupines, you must first attach meaning to an animal that may be unfamiliar to the children. Once you have briefly discussed what a porcupine is, have the children clap the syllables in the word *porcupine*, which in this case can also help with the pronunciation.

- The next step is differentiated depending on the group's control of visual information. One group might be instructed to find the word on the page by looking for the first letter. Then the children should slide their finger under the word while saying it slowly. Another group might be asked to find the word on the page, clap the syllables, and use their fingers to isolate the three syllables in the word (*por-cu-pine*). You may have another group repeat what the other groups did, and then analyze the visual information within each syllable, linking the *r*-controlled vowel in /por/ and the long vowel in /pine/. This is a more detailed visual search that develops an integrated processing system that helps the child use meaning and visual information in tandem.

- Include word work in small-group instruction that teaches children to attend to the details of print. Have children manipulate magnetic letters or letter tiles to emphasize the visual detail with words that are similar. For example, have children change a word's onset while retaining its rime. If *day* is known, first have the children break the word by onset and rime (*d-ay*) and then blend it back together. Next, have the children exchange the onset to make new words that retain the known rime (e.g. *day* to *play* to *stay*). To increase the challenge, have the group retain an onset, such as *st*, while changing the rime: *stand* to *start* to *store*. This type of word work encourages children to look beyond the initial letter or letter combination, and visually search left to right across the entire word.

- Select two letter combinations or patterns the children need to learn, based on your analysis of their errors. Distribute an analogy chart template (scholastic.com/ResourcesNSFRR) inserted in a plastic sheet protector, a dry-erase marker, and an eraser to each child. At the top of your chart, write two familiar words for each spelling pattern (e.g., *can* and *car*). Children should copy these two words on their own charts and underline the pattern in each word (*can*, *car*). Discuss the sound each pattern makes. Tell children you are going to dictate new words for them to write. They should listen for the pattern in the new word to decide which key word has the same sound. Then they should write the new word under the matching key word and underline the pattern. Randomly dictate three or four words for each pattern. As children grow in proficiency, dictate words with inflectional endings. Before they leave the table, have them read the words in each column. This makes the activity both a reading and writing task.

*scholastic.com/ResourcesNSFRR*

| | | | |
|---|---|---|---|
| c<u>an</u> | c<u>ar</u> | ni<u>ght</u> | <u>oi</u>l |
| f<u>an</u> | f<u>ar</u> | br<u>ight</u> | b<u>oi</u>l |
| sc<u>an</u> | sc<u>ar</u> | mi<u>ght</u>y | c<u>oi</u>led |
| b<u>an</u>d | b<u>ar</u>k | flashl<u>ight</u> | unsp<u>oi</u>led |

*Analogy chart for* an *and* ar

*Analogy chart for two complex vowel patterns*

## Whole-Group Instruction

- During shared reading on an enlarged text, conceal a word at the end of a sentence with a sticky note. Then have children read the sentence and predict the word. Chart their predictions, and, from there, reveal the word's initial letter or letter combination. Have children compare the letter or letter combination to the list of predicted words. Continue to reveal the word, attending to the visual detail, and compare that information to the visual detail in the predicted words.

- During interactive or shared writing, post two charts, one for writing a negotiated text and one for engaging in related word work and analysis. The word work that stems from interactive and shared writing will change over time as the children become more proficient users of visual information. At first, you may teach the children how to use Elkonin (1973) boxes, commonly referred to as Sound Boxes, for sound analysis. Select a sound regular word that occurs in the negotiated text. Draw a box for each phoneme, not letter. For example, *cat* has three letters and three phonemes, and therefore, you would draw three boxes.

For *boat*, however, there are four letters but only three phonemes and therefore three boxes. When children hear the sounds in *boat*, they will record /b/ /o/ /t/.

The child may only hear and record /o/. After the child is finished recording, the teacher adds the *a*, explaining to the students that adding the 'a' makes the word look right.

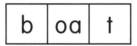

When there is no direct correlation between sound and letter, discuss the importance of balancing phonology (how words sound) and orthography (how words look). As children's use of visual information becomes more sophisticated, and they notice that more than one letter can represent a sound, such as /sh/ in *ship*, /ee/ in *sleep*, or /ar/ in *car*, draw a box for each letter to signal the importance of visual detail and the multiple ways to represent sounds. These are often referred to as letter boxes indicating a letter for each box as opposed to a sound for each box (Clay, 2016).

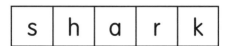

Letter boxes hold children accountable for attending to phonological and orthographic information.

- Develop a key word wall with the class. By "key words," we mean words that the children can use to solve other words with the same parts (e.g., digraphs, blends, rimes, vowel combinations, etc.). Below are suggested lists of key words, organized by part. Whenever possible, use the children's names for key words.

| DIGRAPHS | | BLENDS WITH *R* | | BLENDS WITH *L* | |
|---|---|---|---|---|---|
| Part | Key Word | Part | Key Word | Part | Key Word |
| ch | cheese | br | brown | bl | blue |
| sh | she | cr | cried | cl | class |
| th | the | dr | drive | fl | fly |
| wh | when | fr | frog | gl | glass |
| | | gr | green | pl | play |

| Part | Key Word | Part | Key Word | Part | Key Word | Part | Key Word | Part | Key Word |
|---|---|---|---|---|---|---|---|---|---|
| ai | rain | ea | eat | ie | pie | oa | boat | ue | blue |
| all | ball | ee | see | igh | night | oi | oil | y | happy |
| an | can | er | her | ill | hill | old | old | | |
| and | and | ew | new | ing | king | oo | zoo | | |
| ar | car | | | ir | bird | or | for | | |
| are | care | | | | | ou | out | | |
| at | cat | | | | | ow | cow | | |
| au | because | | | | | ow | snow | | |
| aw | saw | | | | | oy | boy | | |
| ay | play | | | | | | | | |

**Independent Practice**

- Encourage children to read, read, and read some more! Rereading familiar text frees up the brain so that children are more likely to notice aspects of visual information they may not have detected initially. The brain is a pattern seeker, and voluminous reading of continuous text helps build a known reading vocabulary that is strengthened every time a child picks up a book. Because a known reading vocabulary contains units and patterns, it supports children's flexible and generative problem solving in new text.

## CLOSING THOUGHT

Children must understand that there are a variety of ways to use visual information in print. Some words, as discussed in Chapter 9, have to be recognized quickly with little or no attention, while others require a visual analysis. Beginning readers often engage in letter-by-letter analysis, but that should give way to a more complex use of visual information as they attend to the largest and most efficient word units available. Regardless of the type of visual analysis in which children engage, they should always use meaning and structure to assist them.

Sometimes while taking a running record, you may notice that a child's attempt is correct, but that the way he emphasizes the parts of the word provides insight into the attention he gives to the visual information. For example, the child comes to the word *another* and clearly articulates *an* and then says *other*. A simple check on the record shows the child read the word correctly but gives no indication of the real work the child did. This work must be thoroughly recorded and used to make intentional instructional decisions. Ultimately the record serves as a scope and sequence for planning systematic instruction because it documents the information the child used and neglected. Furthermore, it also ensures your instruction addresses the child's or group's needs and that you're not wasting time teaching children what they already know.

## Answer key for the practice activity on pages 173–177:

Accuracy Rate: 95%  Self-Correction Rate: 1:4

| Text | Running Record | Count | | Information Used | |
|------|----------------|-------|---|------------------|---|
| | | **E** | **SC** | **E**<br>**M S V** | **SC**<br>**M S V** |
| Bird needs a new home.<br>She will build a nest!<br>What can Bird use to make the nest? | ✓ $\frac{\text{n-ee-d}}{\text{needs}}$\| ✓ ✓ ✓<br><br>✓ ✓ $\frac{\text{b-✓}}{\text{build}}$ ✓ $\frac{\text{n-e-st}}{\text{nest}}$\| ✓<br><br>$\frac{\text{Wh-at}}{\text{What}}$\|$\frac{\text{w-hat}}{}$\|$\frac{\text{A}}{\text{T}}$\| ✓✓ $\frac{\text{us}}{\text{use}}$ ✓✓✓✓ | 2 | | M S Ⓥ<br><br>M S Ⓥ | |
| Bird finds some sticks in the garden.<br>She can make her nest with sticks! | ✓ $\frac{\text{f-in-d-s}}{\text{finds}}$\|SC ✓ ✓ ✓ ✓ $\frac{\text{g-ar-✓}}{\text{garden}}$<br><br>✓ ✓ ✓ ✓ ✓ ✓ ✓ | | 1 | M S Ⓥ | Ⓜ Ⓢ V |
| Bird sits on the sticks.<br>Does Bird like the sticks?<br>No. The sticks are too sharp. | ✓ ✓ ✓ ✓ ✓<br><br>$\frac{\text{Do-s}}{\text{Does}}$ ✓ ✓ ✓ ✓<br><br>✓ ✓ ✓ ✓ ✓ $\frac{\text{sh-ar-p ✓}}{\text{sharp}}$ | | 1 | M S Ⓥ | |
| Bird finds some hay.<br>She can make her nest with hay! | ✓ ✓ ✓ $\frac{\text{h-✓}}{\text{hay}}$<br><br>✓ ✓ ✓ ✓ ✓ ✓ ✓ | | | | |

| Text | Running Record | Count | | Information Used | |
|---|---|---|---|---|---|
| | | E | SC | E<br>M S V | SC<br>M S V |

Bird sits on the hay.
Does Bird like the hay?
No. The hay is too itchy.

✓ ✓ ✓ ✓

$\dfrac{\text{Do-s} \;|\; SC}{\text{Does} \;|}$ ✓ ✓ ✓ ✓    1    M S Ⓥ   Ⓜ Ⓢ V

✓ ✓ ✓ ✓ ✓ $\dfrac{\text{it-ch} \;|\; \text{itch}}{\text{itchy} \;|}$    1    Ⓜ S Ⓥ

Bird finds some mud.
She can make her nest with mud!

✓ ✓ ✓ ✓

✓ ✓ ✓ ✓ ✓ ✓ ✓

Bird sits in the mud.
Does Bird like the mud?
No. The mud is too messy.

✓ ✓ ✓ ✓ ✓

$\dfrac{\text{Did}}{\text{Does}}$ ✓ ✓ ✓ ✓    1    Ⓜ Ⓢ Ⓥ

✓ ✓ ✓ ✓ ✓ $\dfrac{\text{muddy}}{\text{messy}}$    1    Ⓜ Ⓢ Ⓥ

Bird finds some flowers.
She can make her nest with flowers!

✓ ✓ ✓ ✓

✓ ✓ ✓ ✓ ✓ ✓ ✓

| Text | Running Record | Count E | Count SC | Information Used E M S V | Information Used SC M S V |
|------|----------------|---------|----------|--------------------------|---------------------------|
| Bird sits on the flowers.<br>Does Bird like the flowers?<br>No. The flowers are too big. | ✓ ✓ ✓ ✓ ✓<br><br>Did ✓ ✓ ✓ ✓<br>──<br>Does<br><br>✓ ✓ ✓ ✓ ✓ ✓ | 1 | | Ⓜ Ⓢ Ⓥ | |
| Bird finds some rocks.<br>She can make her nest with rocks! | ✓ ✓ ✓ ✓<br><br>✓ ✓ ✓ ✓ ✓ ✓ ✓ | | | | |
| Bird sits on the rocks.<br>Does Bird like the rocks?<br>No. The rocks are too bumpy. | ✓ ✓ ✓ ✓ ✓<br><br>✓ ✓ ✓ ✓ ✓<br><br>✓✓✓✓✓ jump \|bump\|bumping\|SC<br>　　　　 bumpy\|  \|  \| | 1 | | M S Ⓥ | Ⓜ Ⓢ V |
| Bird is sad.<br>What can she use to make her nest?<br>She will go under the tree.<br>She will think about what to do. | ✓ ✓ mad<br>　　 ──<br>　　 sad | 1 | | Ⓜ Ⓢ Ⓥ | |
| | ✓ ✓ ✓ have ✓ ✓<br>　　　　 ──<br>　　　　 use | 1 | | Ⓜ Ⓢ V | |
| | ✓ ✓ | | | | |
| | ✓ ✓ ✓ ✓ ✓ ✓ | | | | |
| | ✓✓ th-in-k ✓ a-b-out\|aboot\|SC ✓✓✓<br>　　 think　　 about\|  \| | 1 | | M S Ⓥ | Ⓜ Ⓢ V |

| Text | Running Record | Count | | Information Used | |
|---|---|---|---|---|---|
| | | E | SC | E M S V | SC M S V |
| Wait! What is that under the tree? Bird sees grass under the tree. | ✓ ✓ ✓ $\frac{this}{that}$ ✓ ✓ ✓ <br><br> ✓ ✓ ✓ ✓ ✓ ✓ | 1 | | Ⓜ Ⓢ Ⓥ | |
| Bird sits on the grass. Does Bird like the grass? Yes! The grass is soft. Bird can make her nest with grass! | ✓ ✓ ✓ ✓ <br> ✓ ✓ ✓ ✓ <br> ✓ ✓ ✓ ✓ <br> ✓ ✓ ✓ ✓ ✓ ✓ | | | | |
| Bird is happy now. She loves her new nest! | ✓ ✓ ✓ ✓ <br> ✓ $\frac{likes}{loves}$ ✓ ✓ ✓ | 1 | | Ⓜ Ⓢ Ⓥ | |

# Understanding Challenges Identified by Running Record Analysis

In Part IV, we focus on understanding challenges you may uncover through your analysis of running records. For many children, the issues discussed in Chapter 11 will not show up in running records. However, the chapter will be helpful for children whose records indicate a problem after applying the instructional suggestions in Part III. Part IV also contains a chapter on using running records with older striving readers.

 **VIDEO LINK**
Visit **scholastic.com/ResourcesNSFRR** for professional videos of the authors taking, scoring, and analyzing running records.

# CHAPTER 11

# Addressing Specific Issues

In this chapter, we address specific issues you may uncover when working with children. Our years of experience have revealed that these issues must be addressed if we expect children to progress.

When a child is having difficulty, take and analyze running records over the course of two- to four-weeks to identify patterns in his or her processing. Once you have uncovered the patterns, use the teaching suggestions throughout this book to provide targeted instruction. Closely observe the child's response. If you do not see a shift in his or her actions and behaviors, meet with a colleague to discuss the running records and identify next steps. This kind of collaborative problem solving is essential in our work with children.

# ISSUE 1: WHEN CHILDREN APPEAR TO INVENT TEXT

When very young children first engage with books, they often use the pictures to make up their own stories. As they learn that print carries the message and learn about letters and sounds, they begin to realize that what they say must match the words on the page. But some children continue to avoid print and invent text, relying on their language skills and the pictures for support. Examine the running record below for the types of errors the child made, including the insertions and omissions.

**I See Colors by Briar Wilton, Level A**
**Running words: 28**

| Text | Record |
|---|---|
| I see a blue bird. | ✓ ✓ ✓ ✓ ✓ |
| I see a red bug. | ✓ ✓ the/a ✓ ladybug/bug |
| I see a yellow flower. | ✓ ✓ ✓ real/yellow big/- sunflower/flower |
| I see a green tree. | ✓ ✓ the/a -/green grass/tree |
| I see an orange cat. | ✓ ✓ a/an big/orange fat/cat cat's/- tail/- |
| I see a brown dog. | ✓ ✓ ✓ hot/brown ✓ |
| I see colors. | There/I are/see lots/colors of/- pictures/- |
| Child did not point while reading. | |

This record clearly shows that the child is not making a speech-to-print match and is, therefore, inventing text in his desire to make meaning. *I See Colors* is a predictable text. The purpose of predictable text is to provide children with a pattern that supports them in one-to-one correspondence. The child is able to control the language pattern of the first line, *I see a blue bird*, even without pointing to the words. When teaching children to match speech to print, it is important to use a text with a pattern the child can control.

If you have a child who struggles with one-to-one correspondence, use a text with a simple pattern and a few known words. If you can't find an appropriate text, create one. Include the child's name and a familiar high-frequency word or two. Put one short sentence (3–5 words) on each page and add a picture or sticker to illustrate the sentence. Involving the child in the creation of the text will also ensure that it is meaningful.

Here are some sample predictable sentence frames to use with beginning readers.

**[Child's name] sees a** _____. (Engage the child in completing the frame with items of the child's choosing. We recommend the items be related or from a similar group like familiar animals, types of vehicles, or names of superheroes.)

**[Child's name] likes** _____. (food, pets, family member, sports)

**[Child's name] can** _____. (complete with action words)

Here is a sample text using a predictable sentence frame, the child's name, and a high-frequency word. The text was created with the child supplying the action word.

Griff can jump.

Griff can run.

### Tips for Making Books That Support One-to-One Correspondence

- Write the text in black marker. Make sure the writing does not bleed through the page.
- Exaggerate spaces between each word, but don't make individual words too large.
- Let the child quickly illustrate each page with stickers.
- Create a title page with a byline featuring the child's name.
- Consider using commercial blank books so you don't have to create the books yourself. This is a time saver.
- Consider downloading and printing online pre-written and illustrated books that allow you to insert a child's name into a simple sentence.

When selecting or creating text for a child who is inventing the words, be sure it contains a predictable pattern that the child can control. When the child controls the pattern, you can demonstrate clear, crisp pointing under each word, using a hand-over-hand technique to connect the language pattern with the words in the text. For children to attend to print and begin accessing visual information, pointing to each word helps them connect what they are saying to what appears in the text. Demonstrating one-to-one correspondence on simple, one-line text will support children with this basic concept of print. It is important to keep in mind, that once children can match one-to-one, they're ready to move beyond patterned text.

# ISSUE 2: WHEN CHILDREN RELY ON PREDICTABLE OR PATTERNED TEXT AND AVOID LOOKING AT PRINT

If children are presented with a single type of text, they can begin to construct a theory of reading based on the characteristics of that text type. For example, when they read only nonsensical decodable or accountable text, they may begin to think reading is about calling out the words on the page. When they read only predictable text, the repetitive pattern can become a crutch. Children may rely on the pattern without looking closely at the print. So, it is important to give children a variety of text types, while also developing their bank of known words. It is also important to provide instruction in using visual information to decode while making sense of text. Examine the running record below and note what happens when the pattern changes on the last page.

**Big and Little** by Megan Duhamel, Level B
**Running words: 39**

| Text | Record |
|------|--------|
| Look at the big elephant. | ✓ ✓ ✓ ✓ ✓ |
| Look at the little elephant. | ✓ ✓ ✓ ✓ ✓ |
| Look at the big bear. | ✓ ✓ ✓ ✓ ✓ |
| Look at the little bear. | ✓ ✓ ✓ ✓ ✓ |
| Look at the big giraffe. | ✓ ✓ ✓ ✓ ✓ |
| Look at the little giraffe. | ✓ ✓ ✓ ✓ ✓ |
| Look at the big monkey and the little monkey. | ✓ ✓ ✓ ✓ ✓ <br><br> look / and — at / the — a / little — baby / - ✓ |
| After the first page, the child only looked at the pictures. Eyes were off text. | |

In this example, the child made four errors in the 39-word text, with an accuracy rate of 89.7 percent, which we round to 90 percent. While it seems as if the child can read this text, his self-correction rate (0:4) and failure to monitor when the text pattern changed indicates that teaching is needed. The record clearly shows, based on his substitutions on the final page, that the child is using the repetitive nature of the text to avoid looking at print. Furthermore, based on the teacher's anecdotal notes, the child's eyes weren't always on the text. His overreliance on the pattern may be due to the lack of known words. Based on his reading of the first six pages, you may assume he knows *look, at,* and *the,* but his reading of the final pages reveals he does not have those words completely under control.

This example illustrates why it's critical to analyze the entire running record and not just part of it. It's also critical to look beyond accuracy rate. In this case, if we only use accuracy rate to make decisions about the text level the child should be reading, we run the risk of keeping him in this type of text for too long. Selecting early-level texts can be challenging, but doing it carefully and wisely will help prevent children from over-relying on the pattern.

### Tips for Selecting Early-Level Text

- Be sure the text contains known words.

- When the pattern changes, the child should know the first word of the sentence.

- Before a child starts reading, remind her that it's okay to glance at the pictures, but once she begins to read, her eyes should stay on the print.

- Select books in which the print is clearly separate from the pictures. For example, the print is on the right page and the picture is on the left. This makes it easier for you to see if the child is looking at the words.

- Be aware that in the early-level texts, not only is the pattern predictable, but unknown words are usually represented in the illustrations. To encourage cross-checking, some of the concepts in the pictures should have synonyms, such as *horse/pony, flower/rose, dog/puppy.* This requires the child to use both the picture and the initial letter to figure out the word. Before a child reads, say, for example, "The word could be *horse* or *pony.* You will have to check the word to see what looks right."

## ISSUE 3: WHEN CHILDREN HAVE DIFFICULTY CONTROLLING SERIAL ORDER

Children who struggle to attend to letters and sounds from left to right across a word have serial-order difficulties. For beginning readers, controlling serial order is a behavior that has to be learned. For older readers, serial-order difficulties can signal other issues. To uncover serial-order issues, analyze the reader's substitutions. Are some of the letters represented but not in the correct sequence? For example, a child with serial-order difficulties may read *play* for *help*, *said* for *and*, and *is* for *said*. Examine the running record below and note errors that may indicate an issue with serial order. One instance on a single running record should not cause alarm, but a consistent pattern of using visual information out of order needs to be addressed.

### Excerpts from *Danny Helps Dad* by Carlos Jimenez, Level E
### Running words: 104

| Page | Text | Record |
|------|------|--------|
| 6 | Danny helps Dad shop at the store.<br><br>"I will push the cart," said Danny. | ✓ please ✓ shops ✓ ✓ ✓<br>   helps     shop<br><br>✓ ✓ hold ✓ ✓ ✓ ✓<br>      push |
| 7 | Danny helps Dad make soup.<br><br>"I will put in the carrots," said Danny. | ✓ please \| SC ✓ cook ✓<br>  helps  \|     make<br><br>✓ ✓ tap ✓ ✓ ✓ ✓ ✓<br>    put |
| 8 | What does Danny do next?<br><br>He gives the soup to Mom.<br><br>"Thanks. I will feel better soon,' said Mom. | That ✓ ✓ ✓<br>What<br><br>✓ ✓ ✓ ✓ ✓<br><br>✓ ✓ ✓ ✓ ✓ ✓ ✓ |

The error pattern shows the child is using the last letter(s) to begin the word instead of the first letter(s), as indicated by the highlighting:

**please, tap, and hold.**
helps    put    push

### Tips for Helping Children With Serial-Order Difficulties

* Use Elkonin boxes to help the child control a left-to-right sound/letter analysis (see Chapter 10). Once the child has written the letters in the boxes, have her write the word without the boxes, making sure she says the word slowly as she writes. Be direct in your teaching, Say, "When you write this word, you have to write the first sound first. If you see this word in a book, show me where you need to look first. Now slide your finger under the word and read it." Make sure the child slides her finger from left to right.

* Slowly slide a card across a word from left to right as the child reads the word.

* Have the child construct a word with magnetic letters and then locate the first letter.

* When a child is writing a word that has been problematic, make sure she writes the first letter first, and be ready to intervene if she doesn't. Writing the word correctly once or twice is usually not enough; they will likely need to practice it many times. Have the child write it in different places (e.g., in a notebook, on a dry-erase board) to send a message that the letter order remains consistent regardless of where the word appears.

* When a child is reading and comes to a word that has been causing confusion, isolate the first letter and/or articulate the first sound.

# ISSUE 4: WHEN CHILDREN DON'T USE THE VISUAL INFORMATION AVAILABLE

The use of visual information develops along a continuum. Through phonics instruction and voluminous reading, children will notice and use more details in words. When children are attending to visual information at the beginning of a word but ignoring letters that follow, they may make an error such as reading *house* for *home*. At emergent reading levels, you may choose to ignore this type of error because it makes sense and begins with the correct letter. However, these errors have to be addressed so that they don't result in a pattern of inefficient and problematic processing. Examine the running record below and identify the type of visual information the child is relying on and the type she is neglecting.

**Excerpts From *The Lemonade Stand* by Jane Brennan, Level J**
**Running words: 388**

| Page | Text | Record |
|------|------|--------|
| 10 | Their next customer was Mrs. Finch.<br><br>She worked at the library.<br><br>"My goodness, it's hot!" said Mrs. Finch<br><br>"I would love a lemonade. In fact, make<br><br>it two." | The \|SC ✓ ✓ ✓ ✓ Fick<br>Their\|             Finch<br><br>✓ ✓ ✓ ✓ ✓<br><br>✓ ✓ ✓ ✓ ✓ ✓ Fick/Finch<br><br>✓ ✓ ✓ ✓ ✓ ✓ ✓<br><br>✓ ✓ |
| 11 | "We don't have change," Matt said.<br><br>"Oh, dear," said Mrs. Finch. "I'll come back<br><br>and pay you tomorrow." | ✓ ✓ ✓ ✓ ✓<br><br>✓ ✓ ✓ ✓ Fick/Finch ✓ ✓ ✓<br><br>✓ ✓ ✓ tonight/tomorrow |

| Page | Text | Record |
|---|---|---|
| 15 | "We're almost out of lemonade," said Matt. "And we haven't made a cent!" Emma cried. Just then their dad walked up. "Can I have a lemonade?" he asked. He drank the very last glass. | ✓ also ✓ ✓ ✓ ✓<br>—almost—<br><br>✓ ✓ ✓ ✓ ✓ ✓ ✓ called<br>—cried—<br><br>✓ ✓ ✓ ✓ ✓ ✓ ✓ ✓<br><br>✓ ✓ ✓ ✓<br><br>✓ drinks ✓ ✓ ✓<br>—drank— |
| 16 | "You've worked really hard today," their dad said. "Why don't I take you out for a special treat? What should it be?" "Ice cream!" they shouted together. So Emma and Matt finally got their ice cream. And it tasted so good. | ✓ ✓ real ✓ ✓ ✓<br>—really—<br><br>✓ ✓ ✓ ✓ ✓ ✓ ✓ ✓<br><br>✓ super ✓ ✓ ✓ ✓ ✓<br>—special—<br><br>✓ ✓ ✓ ✓ ✓<br><br>✓ ✓ ✓ ✓ fin-all │A│ ✓ ✓<br>—finally— │ │T<br><br>✓ ✓ ✓ ✓ ✓ ✓ ✓ |

The child maintains meaning for the most part, but she is missing the nuances of the story. This will negatively affect comprehension. For example, the text says, "I'll come back and pay you tomorrow," but the child reads, "I'll come back and pay you tonight." This integrated error does not change the meaning drastically, but there is definitely a difference between *tonight* and *tomorrow*. The difference should be brought to the child's attention and corrected.

Integrated errors occur when a child fails to monitor using additional visual information to confirm or discount her initial attempt. That may happen because she has not been taught to monitor using visual information or doesn't know the salient parts in the word. When we prompt a child to problem-solve using only the initial letter/sound and/or using meaning and only some visual information, we must encourage her to take the next step: confirm using *all* available visual information.

Once you identify this as an issue, adapt your instruction.

**Tips for Helping Children Search and Use Visual Information**

- Select texts that provide opportunities for children to substitute words using partial visual information while maintaining meaning—for example, substituting *raced* for *ran*. Once you've selected the text, make sure that these types of words are deliberately left for the child to solve and are not used in the book introduction.

- When you anticipate that the child is coming to a challenging word, be ready to intervene. If, for example, the word begins with *st*, isolate the beginning visual information with your finger, and cover the rest of the word. Ask the child not to guess the word. Then expose the next part of the word so he uses additional visual information.

- Show children words with the same initial visual information—for example, *today*, *tonight*, and *tomorrow* or *into*, *inside*, and *instead*. This type of word work forces the child to look beyond the initial letter(s) or part and use additional visual information.

# ISSUE 5: WHEN CHILDREN DEPEND ON THE BOOK INTRODUCTION FOR LANGUAGE AND VOCABULARY

Sometimes children listen intently to our book introductions for language and vocabulary and then use what they remember to avoid problem solving when reading. Typically, this has more to do with the teacher than the student. She may doubt the children's problem-solving abilities, be focused too heavily on accuracy, or feel pressure to move the children to the next text level. So, she unintentionally crafts book introductions that leave no reading work for the children. In essence, she leaves no opportunities for the child to problem-solve. It is only because of the amount of support from the teacher that children are able to read at this level. The surprise comes when the teacher administers a benchmark assessment, and the independent reading level is much lower than expected.

During the book introduction on page 9, the teacher drew the child's attention to the sticky pads on the frog's special feet, overemphasizing this concept and the associated vocabulary. She repeated several times "Frogs have *sticky pads* on their feet and their *special feet* help them go *straight up a window.* '*Straight up a window.*' Do you see the *sticky pads?* And look at their *special feet.*" Given the teacher's comments, notice what happened when the child read the page.

## Excerpts From *Frogs and Toads Are Cool Creatures* by Megan Duhamel, Level J

| Text | Record |
|---|---|
| There are little frogs. This tree frog is the | ✓ ✓ ✓ ✓ ✓ ✓ ✓ ✓ |
| size of a dime. It has little sticky pads on | ✓ ✓ ✓ ✓ ✓ ✓ ✓  special ∣ straight ✓ ✓ <br> sticky ∣ |
| its feet. A tree frog's special feet help it | ✓ ✓ ✓ ✓ ✓  sticky ✓ ✓ ✓ <br> special |
| climb straight up a window. | ✓  - ∣ A ∣ ∣ sticky ✓ ✓ ✓ <br> straight ∣ Y ∣ |

Because of the teacher's introduction, the child expects the words *sticky*, *special*, and *straight* to appear on page 9, which shifts his attention to recalling instead of problem solving. When he encounters unknown words that begin with an *s*, he recalls the words the teacher introduced and uses them. He doesn't engage in further visual analysis that would have resulted in accurate reading.

Use the information in the chart on the next page to craft your book introductions. The suggestions will help you identify places where the children should problem-solve. The introduction should provide enough to support the readers' success while simultaneously leaving important opportunities to problem-solve.

## Crafting Book Introductions

| How will the text support the children? | What must the children control to read the text? | What are the children's opportunities to engage in problem solving in the text? | How will I support the children if they get to a word and stop or are unable to solve after an attempt(s)? | How will I introduce the text? What unfamiliar vocabulary, new concepts, and unusual structures need to be addressed? |
|---|---|---|---|---|
| Identify vocabulary and concepts that are familiar to the children. Known vocabulary and concepts do not need to be included in the introduction.<br><br>For example, on page 9 of *Frogs and Toads Are Cool Creatures*:<br><br>Children understand the meaning of the words *sticky*, *special*, and *straight* and use them in their speaking vocabulary. At this text level, the children should be able to decode these words and extract meaning as they apply their understandings to the features and function of the frog's feet. Telling words like *sticky*, *special*, and *straight* reduces the opportunities children have to integrate meaning, language, and decoding skills. | Using previous running records from the children, locate pages or sections of the text that the children will read without assistance. This decision should be grounded in your observation of what the children know and control. They should not be overwhelmed by problem-solving; instead, you should preview the text to ensure a balance between problem-solving opportunities and words and concepts that are well within the children's control. Don't introduce words students can't figure out on their own.<br><br>For example, there are a number of known high-frequency words on page 9. Word automaticity reduces the cognitive load and frees the children up to use and construct meaning and engage in visual analysis as needed. | Examine each page and determine where the children will problem-solve.<br><br>For example, on page 9, the children will need to decode *sticky* and *straight*. Their knowledge and understanding of these words will assist in their decoding efforts. | Determine the connections or links the children have to the words you expect them to problem-solve.<br><br>For example, on page 9, for *sticky*, the children could use *st* and the known word *sick*. For *straight*, the children know the blend *str* and might try the short-*a* sound. Be ready, to prompt them to try the long vowel sound for /ai/. | Share a sentence or two that summarizes the book. Then go to specific pages as needed to draw attention to the unfamiliar vocabulary, new concepts, and unusual structures.<br><br>For example, on page 9, the word *special* may be difficult to decode. Use the word in the introduction, and then have the children find the word on the page and slide their finger under the word to see the parts. |

| Crafting Book Introductions | | | | |
| --- | --- | --- | --- | --- |
| How will the text support the children? | What must the children control to read the text? | What are the children's opportunities to engage in problem solving in the text? | How will I support the children if they get to a word and stop or are unable to solve after an attempt(s)? | How will I introduce the text? What unfamiliar vocabulary, new concepts, and unusual structures need to be addressed? |
| | | | | |

# ISSUE 6: WHEN CHILDREN'S ACCURACY RATE IS HIGH, BUT THEIR COMPREHENSION IS LIMITED

From time to time, you may have a child with a high accuracy rate but limited comprehension. When this occurs, the running record may look perfect. Don't let numbers fool you! Always engage students in a discussion of the book after they read it.

If a child seems to have limited understanding of the book, record your observations of what is difficult for the child. Perhaps he or she has trouble with the sequence of events, recalling facts, or making inferences. Perhaps the child lacks the background knowledge and experiences to understand the concepts or connect with the characters. Noting your observations will allow you to support comprehension during the introduction of the text by drawing attention to and setting anticipatory expectations for important ideas. Being aware of comprehension issues will also help you scaffold the child during the reading. Use quick comments to support the child's understanding of such issues as sequencing events. For example, as the child turns the page while reading, say, "Let's see what happens next." Making the comment as the child turns the page ensures that you do not interrupt the reading but at the same time prompts the child to think about the text.

Children with high accuracy rate and limited comprehension are often referred to as word callers. Drawing attention to meaning before, during, and after reading will support a child's construction of meaning and comprehension of the text and prevent children from thinking that reading is simply about calling out the words. More information on limited comprehension with older, striving readers is discussed in Chapter 12.

## CLOSING THOUGHT

We admit that finding time to complete a running record isn't always easy. Sometimes teachers take the record but don't score and analyze it. However, doing all three steps uncovers specific problems and can guide your instruction. Running records give you the opportunity to reflect on your teaching and on the children's learning. We *challenge* you to take the extra steps needed to complete the running record fully. Meeting this challenge will provide great insight and assist you in supporting readers in powerful ways.

# CHAPTER 12

# Using Running Records With Intermediate Striving Readers

The running records we've shown you so far are from early and transitional readers in the primary grades. Now we'll discuss running records from older students. Classroom teachers commonly take running records three times a year as benchmark measures for students, but with older students reading below grade level, it's tremendously beneficial to take a running record every couple weeks as part of the instructional cycle. Taking running records more frequently allows you to analyze the student's reading process, monitor progress, and plan your next instructional steps.

## ALL READERS MAKE ERRORS

Fluent readers, including adults, often make errors, especially when reading rapidly. They may ignore types of words such as articles, substitute a word that makes sense, make an error and correct it, or ignore an error if it doesn't change the meaning of the passage. Consider the last time you read aloud in public. Did you read the text with 100 percent accuracy? Chances are, if someone had taken a running record on you, they would have recorded a few errors and self-corrections. Although an occasional error isn't a problem for proficient readers, a pattern of errors can signal a problem with a striving reader's processing system.

For older students needing reading intervention, the best way to identify a pattern of errors is to take a running record, which takes only a few minutes if you use a short passage (100–150 words). It is a few minutes well spent, because the assessment provides a wide range of valuable information such as text accessibility, problem-solving behaviors, knowledge and application of phonics skills, vocabulary, fluency, and—when followed by a short conversation about the passage—comprehension. Armed with "in-the-moment" knowledge, you can plan a targeted lesson that will address the student's specific reading issues.

The following running record was taken on David, a middle school student Jan has been teaching. David qualifies for special education services due to a learning disability. He's had an IEP since first grade and was recently diagnosed with dyslexia. When Jan started working with him, he was reading at text Level M (second grade). After six weeks of instruction that included 32 lessons, David accelerated to Level Q (fourth grade). For each lesson, Jan had David read a new short text and engage in word study. She also took a running record on the short text David read in a previous lesson. The information Jan gleaned from the running record helped her target the skills and strategies David needed to move forward as a reader.

Using David's running record on the next page, we will walk you through the process of assessing a reader's strengths and needs, making instructional decisions, and guiding this older striving reader to become a better reader. David read *Flying Spies* by Ellen Lewis (Level Q), which explains how soldiers used pigeons as spies during World War I.

| Accuracy rate = 95%  SC rate = 1:3 | Running Record | E | SC |
|---|---|---|---|
| A soldier stuffed a note in a tube and | ✓✓ sniffed \|SC ✓ ✓ ✓ ✓ ✓<br>___sniffed___<br>stuffed \| | (M)(S)V | M S(V) |
| tied it to Cher Ami's leg. During her | ✓ ✓ ✓ ✓ Ami ✓. ✓ ✓<br>___Ami___<br>Ami's | (M)(S)(V) | |
| flight, Cher Ami was shot. Somehow | ✓ ✓ ✓ ✓ ✓ . ✓ | | |
| she was able to keep flying even | ✓ ✓ ✓ ✓ ✓ ✓ | (M)(S)(V) | |
| though she was badly injured. | through ✓ ✓ ✓ ✓ .<br>though | | |
| Cher Ami delivered her message, and | ✓ ✓ ✓ ✓ ✓ ✓ | | |
| 200 men were saved! | ✓ ✓ ✓ ✓! | (M)(S)(V) | |
| Cher Ami almost died. Doctors saved | ✓ ✓ ✓ ✓ . ✓ ✓ | (M)(S)(V) | M S(V) |
| her life, but she lost one of her legs. | ✓ ✓ , ✓ ✓ ✓ ✓ ✓ ✓ . | M (S)(V) | |
| The doctors made her a wooden leg | ✓ doctor ✓ ✓ ✓ ✓<br>___doctor___<br>doctors | M S (V) | |
| to replace it. She was given | ✓ represent \|R\|SC ✓. ✓ ✓ ✓<br>___represent___<br>replace \| \| | | |
| a medal for her bravery. She became | ✓ model ✓ ✓ ✓ . ✓ ✓<br>___model___<br>medal | | |
| so famous that her body was preserved | ✓ ✓ ✓ ✓ ✓ ✓ per-saved \|R<br>___per-saved___<br>preserved \| | | |
| after she died. It is on display at a | ✓ ✓ ✓ . ✓ ✓ ✓ ✓ ✓ | | |
| museum in Washington, DC. | ✓ ✓ ✓ ✓ . | | |

(100 words)

# USE RUNNING RECORDS TO MAKE INSTRUCTIONAL DECISIONS

Follow these five steps to maximize your understanding of an older striving reader and make instructional decisions.

## Step 1: Determine the Accuracy Level and Self-Correction Rate

Divide the number of words read accurately, including self-corrections, by the total number of words in the passage. This will give you a percentage. As a rule of thumb, if the student's accuracy rate is between 95 and 100 percent, the text is good for independent reading. An easy-to-read text allows students to focus on comprehending the book. If the accuracy rate is between 90 and 94 percent, the text will work well for guided reading because it contains enough challenge to provide instructional opportunities. If the accuracy rate is below 90 percent, the text level is too difficult for independent reading or guided reading.

### *Instructional Implications*

Be flexible and use your good judgment when matching readers to texts, keeping in mind that a student might be able to read a more challenging text than the accuracy rate suggests. Not all errors should be treated equally. For instance, students learning English may struggle with proper nouns and unfamiliar vocabulary. You should take that into account when evaluating the appropriateness of a text. It is also common for readers to drop word endings. Although that is considered an error, it seldom interferes with comprehension. Furthermore, if a student has a great deal of background knowledge about a topic or shows a keen interest in a book, he or she may be able to independently read it, even if his or her accuracy rate for text at that book's level suggests otherwise.

| When the accuracy rate is | The text is appropriate for |
| --- | --- |
| 95–100% | Independent reading and literature circles |
| 90–94% | Guided reading |
| Below 90% | Read-aloud and shared reading |

## Next Steps for David

On the second reading of *Flying Spies*, David read with 95 percent accuracy and a self-correction rate of 1:3. Although 95 percent accuracy is the bottom threshold of the independent level, Level Q texts are probably more appropriate for David's guided reading instruction. When reading on his own, David should be matched with books one or two levels below Q so he can focus on the content and enjoy the book. Easy-to-read books develop student confidence, promote fluency, and support comprehension.

# Step 2: Analyze Errors and Self-Corrections: MSV

Circle M if you believe the student used meaning at the point of error, circle S if the student used language structure, and circle V if the reader used visual information. To determine whether the student used meaning, reread the sentence and ask, "Does the substitution make sense?". Most striving readers in the upper grades use meaning, structure, and some visual information. Errors most often result when the student ignores some of the letters in the word.

## Instructional Implications

In deciding how to help the student, it is important to look for patterns of errors. In the chart below, we present the most common error patterns that occur with older striving readers. In addition to the error pattern, you'll find an example, the processing issue, and instructional guidelines for correcting the problem.

| Error Pattern | Example | Processing Issue | Instructional Guidelines |
|---|---|---|---|
| **Uses visual information at the beginning of the word and says a word that would make sense** | represent‌ / replace | Not attending to detail within the word | During guided instruction, say, "That makes sense, but does it look right? Check the word with your finger and say it slowly. What would look right?".<br><br>Use word study activities that teach the student to look closely at the parts of a word. Dictate a multisyllabic word from the story. Have the student repeat the word as she claps the syllables. Then have her make the word with magnetic letters. Next, tell the student to break apart groups of letters to show the syllables or the morphemes.<br><br>e.g., *interaction*<br><br>*in ter ac tion*<br><br>*inter action* |

| Error Pattern | Example | Processing Issue | Instructional Guidelines |
|---|---|---|---|
| **Uses some visual information but says a nonsense word** | *per-saved* <br> *preserved* | Broke the word apart but read the parts incorrectly. He may need phonics instruction on *r*-controlled vowels and prefixes. | Following phonetic rules does not always result in correct pronunciation. Phonetic pronunciation must be checked against the meaning of the sentence and paragraph. After the student breaks the word apart, prompt him to reread the sentence and think of a word that makes sense and looks right. <br><br> Use word study activities to teach needed phonics skills. Dictate words with similar vowel patterns and have students write them. As students become more proficient with the vowel pattern, dictate words with inflectional endings and affixes. Here is an example of a word study activity that uses an analogy chart to teach vowel patterns. <br><br> girl            car <br><br> third          started <br><br> firmly       harmful <br><br> confirmed   charmingly |
| **Uses visual information but ignores meaning** | *model* <br> *medal* | Didn't notice the substitution wasn't meaningful. Needs to monitor for meaning. | During guided reading and independent instruction, if the student makes a meaning-changing error, say, "Did that make sense?". Then prompt the student to reread the sentence to fix the error. |
| **Uses visual information, meaning, and structure but ignores the ending** | *doctor* <br> *doctors* | Not noticing the end of words | During guided reading or individual lessons, prompt the student to check the end of the word. Say, "Check here," as you place the tip of your pencil on the ending. <br><br> Use word study activities that require children to attend to the details in words. <br><br> Students can make a word with magnetic letters and add different inflectional endings. <br><br> (e.g., *digest – digests – digested – digesting*) |

## Next Steps for David

Upon close inspection of David's running record on page 211, notice that he used meaning, structure, and visual information at the point of error and used additional visual information to self-correct. Having taken numerous running records on David, Jan concludes that two patterns surface in David's errors:

- He always attends to the beginning of a word, but he frequently ignores the sequence of letters in the middle or end.

- He is missing some foundational skills. In this running record, he struggles with the r-controlled vowel and the prefix *pre-*. A review of his last few running records reveals some other phonics deficiencies.

The following chart presents some of David's errors, the phonics skills he lacks, and the steps Jan took to teach him those skills.

| Errors | Phonics Skills Needed | Next Steps for Instruction |
|---|---|---|
| reply<br>repair<br><br>reported<br>repeated<br><br>planet<br>plain<br><br>croaks<br>crooks<br><br>clock<br>cloak | Vowel patterns: *ai, ea, ee, aw, er, ir, ur* | **Use magnetic letters to teach the vowel patterns.**<br><br>For example, to teach the r-controlled vowels, the students should write or use magnetic letters to make and read these words: *shark – shirk – smirk - shirt –smart*.<br><br>Use analogy charts to teach words with similar vowel patterns. Model the *ai* sound with *rain* and *aw* sound with the known word *saw*. Then dictate other words that have one of those patterns. The student identifies the vowel sound, writes the word under the correct column, and underlines the vowel pattern. |

rain            saw

stain           straw

waited          awful

container       squawking

| Errors | Phonics Skills Needed | Next Steps for Instruction |
|---|---|---|
| waggly<br>waggle<br><br>blossoming<br>blossoms<br><br>busted<br>bustling<br><br>visit<br>visited | Inflectional endings: *le, ly, ing, s, ed* | **Make a card for each target ending.**<br>First, display the ending cards and have the students read them. Then dictate words for the students to write that contain the target endings. Before writing the word, prompt the students to repeat the word and emphasize the ending so it is easier to hear it.<br><br>le    ly<br><br>Dictate: *wiggly, shortly, orderly, squarely, unkindly, carefully*<br><br>Dictate: *little, shuttle, brittle, ripple, squiggle, throttle, sprinkle* |
| independed<br>indentured<br><br>danger<br>dangerous<br><br>infective<br>infection<br><br>equal<br>equality<br><br>officer<br>official | Suffixes: *-ture, -ous, -tion, -ity, -tial, -cial, -able, -ive* | **Make a card for each target affix.**<br>First, display the affix cards and have the students read them. Then dictate words for the students to write or make with magnetic letters. Have students clap the syllables before they write or make the word. This helps them hear each part, so they are more successful in writing the word.<br><br>tion    cial    ity<br><br>Dictate: *relation, vacation, intention, invention, promotion, constitution, infection, relation*<br><br>Dictate: *facial, racial, special, crucial, social, superficial, artificial*<br><br>Dictate: *activity, quality, gravity, equity, cavity, ability, humanity* |

Although an analysis of errors naturally focuses attention on a student's needs, it is important to also look for a student's strengths. You can do that by asking yourself what may have caused the student to self-correct. In David's running record of his reading of *Flying Spies*, he corrected two mistakes. Let's examine those two self-corrections to look for strengths.

| Student's Reading | Strengths |
|---|---|
| sniffed\|SC<br>A soldier stuffed a note in a tube… | David looked at the next word and realized *sniffed* didn't make sense. He was then able to use additional visual information to correct his error. |
| represent\|SC<br>The doctors made her a wooden leg to replace it. | A wooden leg could "represent" a real leg, so David was using meaning. Most likely he recognized the known word *place* and used it to correct the error. |

## Step 3: Analyze Problem-Solving Behaviors

Look beyond the errors and identify behaviors the reader exhibited to solve challenging words. Here are the most visible problem-solving behaviors of striving readers in the intermediate grades:

- **Stopping because they noticed something wasn't right.** This is a sign of monitoring. A reader who doesn't stop at an error won't be able to correct it.

- **Repeating the word.** A student often repeats a word to confirm if the response is correct or to get a better look at the visual information.

- **Rereading to gather more information.** A student might reread the sentence and decode the unknown word by searching for a meaningful context.

- **Saying the unknown word in parts.** The student might break apart the word by syllable, base word and inflectional ending, known part, onset and rime, or affix and root word.

- **Using the illustrations**. If the text has photographs or drawings, the reader might look to them to access the meaning of the word and decode it correctly.

- **Appealing for help**. Although asking for the teacher's assistance is a sign of monitoring, the instructional goal is for the student to attack the word independently.

## Instructional Implications

Stopping, repeating, rereading, saying a word in parts, and using the illustrations are all effective actions students can take when they encounter unfamiliar words. Explicitly teach those strategies so students know what to do when they come to unknown words. When conferring with a student who has problems with decoding, prompt him or her to try one of the strategies you have taught. Praise attempts even when they don't result in accurate reading. With praise, as well as prompting, students will internalize the strategies and behaviors to become more proficient readers.

Some students appeal for help as a first option. This is not useful. Remind them that they need to do their best to work on hard words. However, it is okay for them to ask for help after they have exhausted their repertoire of strategic actions. Although we always want students to take the initiative to solve unknown words, there will be occasions when they just can't figure them out. For example, Luke, a sixth-grade student, was reading the word *conscience*. He stopped and said, "I see *con* and *science*. Is it *con science*?" Because *conscience* wasn't part of his working vocabulary, the teacher had to tell him the word and explain its meaning.

## Next Steps for David

On David's running record, we see evidence of several problem-solving behaviors. He stops, repeats an error, says the word in parts, and self-corrects if he can phonetically access the word. To increase his accuracy rate, he needs to monitor more closely for meaning and attend to the parts of multisyllabic words.

Jan recounts that once, when she was working with David, he stopped at the word *comfortable*. He meticulously broke the word into parts and said, *com – for – table*. Even after he reread the sentence to access context, the word *comfortable* didn't enter his mind. When she finally told him the word was *comfortable*, he gave her a puzzled look and said, "That's *comtable*? Why is there an *f* in it?" Because he had always mispronounced *comfortable*, he didn't recognize it in text.

## Step 4: Assess Vocabulary Knowledge

As students cross the threshold into the fluent reading stage (Levels Q and higher), they will encounter more challenging vocabulary. Some words will be difficult to decode (e.g., *conventionally*, *discrimination)*, and others may not be in their listening vocabulary (e.g., *chortled, bedraggled*). When reading scientific or historic texts, students might stumble on names and countries or content-specific vocabulary, such as *apartheid* and *tsunami*. These kinds of words can present challenges on a running record, and that fact should be considered when determining the text difficulty and planning instruction. If the running record has a lot of content-specific words that are unfamiliar to the student, you might want to take another running record on a text with more familiar vocabulary.

### *Instructional Implications*

Jan is currently doing a virtual book study with three middle school boys, all of whom are striving readers. They are reading *The Merry Adventures of Robin Hood* by Howard Pyle. At their last discussion, she asked them to share words they didn't know. They mentioned *yeoman, bout, christened,* and *enthusiastically. Enthusiastically* was in their listening vocabulary but it was hard to decode. *Bout* was decodable, but the boys weren't familiar with its meaning. *Yeoman* and *christened* were both difficult to decode and new to them.

Always make decisions about text level in light of the student's background knowledge and ability to access the challenging vocabulary. The accuracy rate for one text may not be the same as the rate for another text at the same level. When making instructional decisions about texts and grouping, use running records and your knowledge of the student, along with your good teacher judgment.

Before students read a text during independent or guided reading, introduce new words they probably won't be able to decode. With a multisyllabic word like *enthusiastically*, you might write the word by syllable on a dry-erase board (e.g., *en thu si as tic al ly*). If the text includes unfamiliar scientific or historical terms, discuss them before the student reads them.

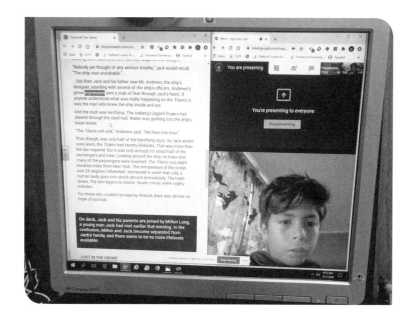

### Next Steps for David

In the running record in this chapter, the only phrase unfamiliar to David was *Cher Ami*, the name of the famous spy pigeon. He often struggles with proper names, even when they are decodable (e.g., *Kayla, Mattie*). He recently read the book *Nelson Mandela* by Caitlin Prozonic (level T). David had never heard of this great civil rights leader, and it took him several tries before he could pronounce Mandela correctly. *Apartheid* was also an extremely challenging word for him. Although he could find *apart* in *apartheid*, he struggled with the last syllable. Jan told him to think about *Tide,* the laundry detergent. That connection did the trick.

Why was *apartheid* so difficult for David? First, it was a new concept for him. Second, he didn't understand how to pronounce *heid*. To further complicate things, David's IEP revealed that he has limited working memory. Just telling him a word isn't enough. He has to create a pathway for remembering it.

It is not uncommon for older striving readers to have difficulty remembering words, and because they don't remember what certain words look like, it's also not uncommon for them to be poor spellers. Some will spell common words phonetically (e.g., *sed* for *said* and *speshal* for *special),* even though they have read those words hundreds of times. It takes intentionality and ingenuity to help some students move items from short-term to long-term memory. The student has to create new neurological pathways for remembering. Because each child is different, you'll need to search for pathways that work for that particular child. Here are some suggestions you can explore and experiment with:

- Link the unknown to the known—Linking *heid* to *Tide* helped him read *apartheid*.
- Make spelling and meaning connections by using something that especially interests the child. One student, for instance, might love vehicles, so it would be easy to teach him how to spell the word *vehicle*. From there, you could make spelling connections to *circle, cycle,* and *miracle,* as well as a meaning connection to *vehicular*.
- Group words with similar features for reading and spelling—*predicting, prediction, predicted, predictors*.
- Use visual analogies—"*Rubble* is like *bubble*."

- Harness the power of repetition, but keep it interesting and engaging. Have students practice writing words with gel pens or on a dry-erase board or an LCD writing tablet.

- Use hands-on activities. Students can make a new word out of magnetic letters, mix up the letters, and then remake it. Any kinesthetic activity can reinforce memory.

- Think of a catchy saying (e.g., *a rat is in sep<u>a</u>rate*; *a <u>pie</u>ce of pie*).

Once students begin creating pathways for remembering, it will take less time for them to learn something new. The important thing is to present the connection so that the child sees it as an easy and fun way to learn.

## Step 5: Assess Fluency and Comprehension

If you have taken running records on older readers, you know it is often difficult to keep up with the student. Most older students read rapidly, but reading rate is only one aspect of fluency. Chapter 6, Checking Fluency and Comprehension, explains each aspect and provides a rubric for rating a student's fluency. Make a note on the running record if you notice that the student struggles with one or more aspects of fluency.

To assess comprehension, we recommend that you follow the running record with a short conversation about the text. You can use generic prompts such as, "What did you read so far?" "What did you learn?" or "What happened in this part of the book?" You might also assess the student on some aspect of comprehension by asking a more specific question. For example, if you want to know if the student needs more instruction on summarizing, you could say, "In two sentences, summarize what you just read." Another option is to ask for specific information that was in the passage. This isn't a test, and your goal isn't to do a complete comprehension survey, but you do need to know if the student has adequate comprehension at the text level you've chosen.

### Instructional Implications

It is a common practice to assess children's reading proficiency by timing how quickly they can read. However, assessing reading speed is an inefficient use of instructional time and can be harmful to developing readers. Children taught that "speed is all you need" may not take the time to correct errors, reread for clarity, or reflect on the meaning of a text. All readers, not just striving ones, need to understand that speed is not the goal. Comprehension is the goal. We want children to read with fluency, but we also want them to read with comprehension. They need both.

**When fluency is a concern.** The first step is to understand why the student isn't fluent. Here are some things to consider:

- The text might be too difficult (evidenced by the accuracy rate).
- The student might lack background knowledge (evidenced by errors on content-specific vocabulary).
- The student might have inefficient word-solving skills (evidenced by decoding errors).
- The student might be ignoring punctuation (evidenced by inappropriate phrasing and pausing).

| If... | Then... |
|-------|---------|
| **the text is too difficult...** | • provide a more supportive introduction during guided reading or choose an easier text.<br>• guide the student to choose an easier text during independent reading. |
| **the student lacks background knowledge on the topic...** | • discuss the topic before the student reads about it.<br>• choose books on familiar topics.<br>• for independent reading, encourage students to choose books they want to read. |
| **the student has inefficient word-solving skills...** | • use the word study activities described in this chapter. For more word study lessons, see *The Next Step Forward in Word Study and Phonics* (Richardson & Dufresne, 2019). |
| **The student ignores punctuation and therefore lacks appropriate intonation...** | • during guided reading, prompt the student to stop and take a breath at each period. If the student runs through the punctuation, place your pencil at the punctuation and say, "Check here. Try that again and use the punctuation." |

Periods, commas, and exclamation points are like road signs for readers. Readers should slow down when they see a dash, stop at a period, and read with excitement when they come to an exclamation point. It's important to pay attention to punctuation because punctuation is directly related to comprehension.

**When comprehension is a concern.** Without comprehension, reading is dull and unrewarding. It's not uncommon for older striving readers to have excellent decoding skills but poor comprehension. You would never suspect they don't have a clue what they're reading! For these readers, focus your instruction on strategies for improving comprehension. (See the next section, Improving Comprehension for Older Striving Readers.)

### *Next Steps for David*

Fluency and comprehension are not the biggest stumbling blocks to David's progress. He is able to retell and discuss what he reads, even when he struggles with the words. David needs to monitor for meaning, improve his knowledge of vowel combinations, inflectional endings, and suffixes, and expand his strategies for decoding challenging words. As Jan systematically takes running records and continues to target David's needs, his decoding will improve. Then he'll be ready to focus more of his attention on analyzing, evaluating, and interacting with the text.

# IMPROVING COMPREHENSION FOR OLDER STRIVING READERS

Although the focus of this book is not comprehension, we want to give you some suggestions for improving comprehension for older striving readers. The following chart lists common standards and comprehension skills, prompts for when you confer with students, and instructional scaffolds students can use while they read. For more detailed information on teaching comprehension, see Chapter 7 of *The Next Step Forward in Guided Reading* (Richardson, 2016).

| Focus | Teacher Prompts | Scaffolds to Use During Reading |
|---|---|---|
| **Monitoring Using Meaning** | *Did that make sense? Read that sentence again and try to figure out that word.* | • Have students mark places in the text where it doesn't make sense to them. Confer with individuals about their confusion. |
| **Monitoring Using Visual Information** | *That makes sense, but does it look right?*<br><br>*Check the word with your finger and see if you can fix it.* | • Have students mark places in the text where they don't know the word. Confer with individuals and teach word-solving strategies and phonics skills they need. |
| **Retelling** | *What did you read? What has happened so far?*<br><br>*What did you learn?*<br><br>*Who is the important character? What did he (or she) do?* | • Have students stop at the end of a page or two and tell themselves what they read.<br><br>• For fiction, have students write a who-what statement that includes the important character and what he or she did.<br><br>• After reading, have students use the fingers on one hand to recall and retell the five story elements.<br><br>**Thumb:** *The characters are…*<br>**Pointer finger:** *The setting is…*<br>**Tall finger:** *The problem is…*<br>**Ring finger:** *The important events are…*<br>(The solution is the last event.)<br>**Little finger:** *At the end…* |

**PART IV**

| Focus | Teacher Prompts | Scaffolds to Use During Reading |
|---|---|---|
| **Developing Vocabulary** | *Is there a word you don't know the meaning of? What can you do to define it?*<br><br>*Can you substitute a word that would make sense in the sentence?*<br><br>*Does the illustration help you?*<br><br>*Reread the sentence. Does that help?*<br><br>*Try reading past the word. Does that help?*<br><br>*Have you heard that word before? Tell me about that.*<br><br>*Is there a part you know in the word?* (point out roots and affixes)<br><br>*Can you connect this word to a similar one you know?* | • Explicitly teach strategies for determining the meaning of unknown words.<br><br>**Vocabulary Strategies**<br>1. Reread (or read on) and look for clues.<br>2. Use the picture to explain the word.<br>3. Use a known part.<br>4. Make a connection.<br>5. Substitute a word that makes sense.<br>6. Use the glossary.<br><br>• Teach students to use illustrations, photographs, charts, diagrams, or other text features to define unknown words.<br><br>• Have students flag or record new words they encounter while reading. During individual or group conferences, discuss the words and the strategies they used to determine the meaning. |
| **Asking and Answering Questions** | *What are you wondering?*<br><br>*What questions do you have?*<br><br>*How are ___ and ___ similar? How are they different?*<br><br>*What caused...?*<br><br>*What was the effect of...?* | • Flag an important paragraph in the text and ask the student to write a question about it.<br><br>• Have students flag an important action, fact, or idea, and write a question about it.<br><br>• Have students take turns asking and answering each other's questions. |

## Improving Comprehension for Older Striving Readers *continued*

| Focus | Teacher Prompts | Scaffolds to Use During Reading |
|---|---|---|
| **Identifying Main Idea and Details** | *What is the central message/main idea?*<br><br>*What reasons or evidence does the author give to support the central message/main idea?*<br><br>*What is the author's point in this section? What details support that point?*<br><br>*What is the most important part of the passage?* | • Teach students to turn a heading or chapter title into a question. This helps them focus on the main idea. Then ask them to record key ideas that answer the main idea question.<br><br>• Have students jot down key words while they read a section or chapter. Then ask them to use the key words to discuss the passage. |
| **Analyzing Characters** | *How does the character feel now? What caused that feeling?*<br><br>*How have the character's feelings changed? What caused the change?*<br><br>*Think about the character's actions. What traits describe the character?*<br><br>*Did [character] change throughout the story? How? What caused the change?*<br><br>*What motivated the character to do (or say) that?* | • Insert sticky notes on a few pages where a character displays a trait. When students come to the sticky note, ask them to write a trait for the character. If necessary, give them a list of traits to choose from.<br><br>• Teach students to flag actions that provide evidence of a character trait.<br><br>• Teach students to flag important actions and write about the motivation behind them.<br><br>• Teach students to use a two-column graphic organizer to record important actions and matching traits or motivations.<br><br>**Action    Trait or Motivation** |

**Improving Comprehension for Older Striving Readers** *continued*

| Focus | Teacher Prompts | Scaffolds to Use During Reading |
|---|---|---|
| **Analyzing Relationships** | *Describe the relationship between _____ and _____. (events, ideas, people, or concepts)*<br><br>*How are _____ and _____ similar? How are they different?*<br><br>*What was the effect of...?*<br><br>*What caused...?*<br><br>*Describe the relationship between (character) and (character).* | • Distribute two sticky flags and ask students to find two concepts that can be compared. Tell them to write a question about the two concepts and answer the question. Students will ask and answer each other's questions during the group discussion.<br><br>• Teach students how to use a sociogram to track the relationships between characters.<br><br>**Create a Sociogram**<br><br>**1.** Identify characters.<br>**2.** Draw circles and lines.<br>**3.** Describe relationships.<br><br>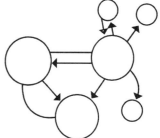 |

| Focus | Teacher Prompts | Scaffolds to Use During Reading |
|---|---|---|
| **Inferring** | *What are you thinking now?*<br><br>*What are you thinking about the character?*<br><br>*Why do you think the character said (or did) that?*<br><br>*What might the character be thinking or feeling right now? Why?*<br><br>*What conclusions can you draw about …?* | • Have students make a T-chart with these headings "In the Text – In my Head." Have them record a fact/event from the book in the first column and their inference in the second.<br><br>**In the Text** / **In My Head**<br><br>Helen didn't speak up to the teacher. / She was embarrassed or maybe ashamed.<br><br>• Have students make a T-chart with these headings "If – Then." As they read, have them create an *If* statement using a fact from the text, and a *Then* statement using their inference.<br><br>(e.g., *If the Sherriff of Nottingham had been more observant, then he would have captured Robin Hood.*) |
| **Summarizing** | *Find three or four key words in the passage to help you summarize it.*<br><br>*Use the main idea and key details to summarize the passage.*<br><br>*Summarize this part in a sentence or two.* | • To summarize fiction, teach students to write a Somebody-Wanted-But-So statement (Macon, Bewell, & Vogt, 1991).<br><br>**Somebody:** Who is the chapter about?<br><br>**Wanted:** What did the character want?<br><br>**But:** What happened?<br><br>**So:** How did the chapter end? What happened next?<br><br>• To summarize nonfiction, teach students to record key words as they read and then use those words to write a sentence or two about the text. |

**Improving Comprehension for Older Striving Readers** *continued*

| Focus | Teacher Prompts | Scaffolds to Use During Reading |
|---|---|---|
| **Comparing and Contrasting Two Texts on the Same Topic** | *Have you read other texts like this?*<br><br>*How does this text compare to _____ (text by the same author or on a similar topic)?*<br><br>*How are _____ and _____ similar and different?* | • Provide question stems students can use while reading two texts on the same topic.<br><br>*How are ___ and ___ similar (or different)?*<br><br>• Have them share their ideas during individual or group conferences. |
| **Using Text Features** | *Why did the author include the map, illustration, or chart on page _____?*<br><br>*What questions can you ask about this map (graph, chart, etc.)?*<br><br>*How do the illustrations contribute to the meaning/mood of the passage?*<br><br>*What can you learn from this text feature?*<br><br>*Read the caption. What new information have you learned?* | • Have students flag a text feature and write why the author included it.<br><br>• Have students flag an illustration, map, or chart and record facts they learned just from the text feature (not the text).<br><br>• Have students prepare questions about a text feature. During group discussion, students can ask and answer each other's questions. |

| Focus | Teacher Prompts | Scaffolds to Use During Reading |
|---|---|---|
| **Evaluating** | *What did you think about this text?*<br><br>*How is this book similar to or different from another book you've read?*<br><br>*What is your opinion? How is it different or similar to the author's?*<br><br>*What are the two sides of the argument? What evidence supports each side?*<br><br>*What lesson did the character learn?*<br><br>*What lesson can you learn from this story?* | • Have students take a fact from the text and turn it into an opinion statement. Discuss the difference.<br><br>• Have students write an email to the author, sharing their thoughts about the text and asking questions.<br><br>• After reading a persuasive text, have students evaluate one side of an argument. Tell them to record key words from the text that support or oppose the argument.<br><br>• Teach students how to determine the theme of a fiction piece.<br><br>**Step 1** Record topics that appear in the story (e.g., love, kindness, hope, trust, integrity, voice, etc.).<br><br>**Step 2** Use one of the topics and write a sentence that begins with *The character learned...* (e.g., *The character learned that she needs to speak up when people treat her unkindly.*)<br><br>**Step 3** Write another sentence about the topic that explains what the author believes. This leads students to the theme (e.g., *People need to stand up for what is right.*). |

## CLOSING THOUGHT

As reading professionals, we know how important it is to invest in early intervention for struggling readers. However, there will always be students in the upper grades who slipped through the cracks. It is never too late. Assess their needs, decide your course of action, and guide them to become better readers.

# REFERENCES

Bishop, R. S. (1990). Mirrors, windows, and sliding glass doors. *Perspectives, 6*(3), ix–xi.

Clay, M. M. (1966). *Emergent reading behaviour* (Doctoral dissertation, ResearchSpace@ Auckland).

Clay, M. M. (2001). *Change over time in children's literacy development*. Heinemann.

Clay, M. M. (2016). *Literacy lessons designed for individuals* (2nd Ed.). Heinemann.

Clay, M. M. (2019). *An observation survey of early literacy achievement* (4th Ed.). Heinemann.

Compton-Lilly, C. F., Mitra, A., Guay, M., & Spence, L. K. (2020). A confluence of complexity: Intersections among reading theory, neuroscience, and observations of young readers. *Reading Research Quarterly*.

Danne, M. C., Campbell, J. R., Grigg, W. S., Goodman, M. J., & Oranje, A. (2005). Fourth-grade students reading aloud: NAEP 2002 special study of oral reading. The Nation's Report Card. NCES 2006–469. *National Center for Education Statistics*.

Davenport, R. (2002). *Miscues not mistakes: Reading assessment in the classroom*. Heinemann.

Dolch, E. W. (1936). A basic sight vocabulary. *The Elementary School Journal, 36*, 456–60. https://doi.org/10.1086/457353

Doyle, M. A. (2019). Marie M. Clay's theoretical perspective: A literacy processing theory. In Alvermann, D. E., Unrau, N. J., Sailors, M., & Ruddell, R. B. (Eds.), *Theoretical models and processes of literacy* (pp. 84–100). Routledge.

Elkonian, D. B. (1973). U. S. S. R. in J. Downing (Ed.), *Comparative reading* (pp. 551–579). Macmillan.

Fried, M. D. (2013). Activating teaching: Using running records to inform teaching decisions. *Journal of Reading Recovery, 13*(1), 5–16.

Fry, E. (1980). The new instant word list. *The Reading Teacher, 34*(3), 284–289. Retrieved September 11, 2020, from http://www.jstor.org/stable/20195230

Hanford, E. (2019, August 22). At a loss for words: How a flawed idea is teaching millions of kids to be poor readers. *APM Reports*. Retrieved from www.apmreports.org/story/2019/08/22/whats-wrong-how-schools-teach-reading

Harris, T. L., & Hodges, R. E. (1995). *The literacy dictionary: The vocabulary of reading and writing*. International Reading Association.

Harvey, S., & Ward, A. (2017). *From striving to thriving: How to grow confident, capable readers*. Scholastic.

Jackson, F. R. (2009). *Outliers: The story of success: Malcolm Gladwell*. Little, Brown and Company.

McGee, L. M., Kim, H., Nelson, K. S., & Fried, M. D. (2015). Change over time in first graders' strategic use of information at point of difficulty in reading. *Reading Research Quarterly, 50*(3), 263–291.

Quinn, J. M., Wagner, R. K., Petscher, Y., Roberts, G., Menzel, A. J., & Schatschneider, C. (2020). Differential codevelopment of vocabulary knowledge and reading comprehension for students with and without learning disabilities. *Journal of educational psychology, 112*(3), 608.

Richardson, J. (2016). *The next step forward in guided reading: An assess-decide-guide framework for supporting every reader*. Scholastic.

Richardson, J., & Dufresne, M. (2019). *The next step forward in word study and phonics*. Scholastic.

Rumelhart, D. E. (1994). Toward an interactive model of reading. In R. B. Ruddell, M. R. Ruddell, & H. Singer (eds.), *Theoretical models and processes of reading*, 864–894.

Schwartz, R. M. (1997). Self-monitoring in beginning reading. *The Reading Teacher, 51*(1), 40–48.

Schwartz, R. M., & Gallant, P. A. (2011). The role of self-monitoring in initial word-recognition learning. In *Multiple perspectives on difficulties in learning literacy and numeracy* (pp. 235–253). Springer.

Schwartz, S., & Sparks, S. D. (2019). How do kids learn to read? What the science says. *Education Week*.

Sirinides, P., Gray, A., & May, H. (2018). The Impacts of Reading Recovery at scale: Results from the 4-year i3 external evaluation. *Educational Evaluation and Policy Analysis, 40*(3), 316–335.

Stephens, D., Harste, J. C., & Clyde, J. A. (2019). *Reading revealed: 50 expert teachers share what they do and why they do it*. Scholastic.

What Works Clearinghouse. (2013). Beginning reading intervention report: Reading Recovery. Washington, DC: Institute of Education Sciences, US Department of Education.

Wixson, K. K., & Lipson, M. Y. (1991). Perspectives on reading disability research. *Handbook of reading research, 2*, 539–570.

# APPENDIX A

# Recording and Scoring Student Behaviors

| Student Behaviors | Definition | How to Record | How to Score |
|---|---|---|---|
| **Frequent Actions** | | | |
| **Correct Response** | Child reads exactly what is in the text | ✓ | No error |
| **Substitution** | Child replaces a word in the text with another word or an attempt | Child's response / Text | One error |
| **Self-Correction** | Child fixes an error with the correct word | SC | No error |
| **Adding and Skipping Words** | | | |
| **Insertion** | Child adds a word not in the text | Word inserted / - | One error |
| **Omission** | Child skips a word | - / Word omitted | One error |

| Student Behaviors | Definition | How to Record | How to Score |
|---|---|---|---|
| **Repetitions and Rereadings** | | | |
| **Repetition of a Correct Response** | Child repeats the word | R | No error |
| **Repetition of a Substitution** | Child repeats the substitution | R | One error |
| **Multiple Repetitions of a Correct Response** | Child repeats the word more than once (number indicates how many times the word is repeated) | $R_2, R_3$ | No error |
| **Multiple Repetitions of a Substitution** | Child repeats the substitution more than once (number indicates how many times the word is repeated) | $R_2, R_3$ | One error, even when the word is repeated more than once |
| **Repetition on more than one word** | Child repeats two or more words together (mark the words that were repeated) | ↓ ‾‾‾‾|R | No error |
| **Repetition on More Than One Word With Self-Correction on the Rereading** | Child self-corrects while rereading (mark the words that were repeated, drop a line facing down where the child self-corrects and label SC) | ↓ ‾‾|‾‾|R  SC | No Error |

| Student Behaviors | Definition | How to Record | How to Score |
|---|---|---|---|
| **Word Analysis and Multiple Attempts** | | | |
| **Decoding Attempt** | Child tries sounds to get to the word | $\dfrac{\text{n- n-}}{\textit{correct word}}$ | No error (if child produces the correct word; one error if child does not produce the correct word) |
| **Multiple Decoding Attempts** | Child makes multiple attempts on the same word | $\dfrac{\text{st - ay} \mid \text{stay - ing}}{\textit{staying}}$ | No error if the child produces the correct word after multiple attempts |
| **Spelling Out a Word** | Child says each letter name | $\dfrac{\textit{G-O}}{\textit{go}}$ | No error (if child says the correct word after spelling it out); Error if child does not say the correct word. |
| **Requests for Help or No Action** | | | |
| **Appeal** | Child asks for help | $\dfrac{\text{A}}{\textit{correct word}}$ | No error (the error is on the Told) |
| **Told** (Correct word is said by the teacher) | The child is unable to continue, and the teacher tells the word. | $\dfrac{\quad\quad}{\text{T}}$ | One error |
| **You Try It** (Said by the teacher) | The teacher says "You try it" if the child makes no attempt and appeals for help. | $\dfrac{\quad\quad}{\text{Y}}$ | No error |

## RUNNING RECORD

**Student:**                                  **First Language:**              **English Language Level:**

**Teacher:**                                                                    **Date:**

**Text Title:**                               **Level:**                        **Running Words (RW):**

**Accuracy Rate:** _____%     Formula: $\dfrac{RW - E}{RW} \times 100$     **Self-Correction Rate:** ___:___     Formula: $\dfrac{SC}{E + SC}$

**Notes/Observations on Reading Behaviors and Strategic Actions:**

| Page # | Running Record | | Count | | Information Used | |
|---|---|---|---|---|---|---|
| | | | E | SC | E<br>M S V | SC<br>M S V |

## RUNNING RECORD

| Page # | Running Record | Count | | Information Used | |
|--------|----------------|-------|----|------------------|----|
| | | E | SC | E | SC |
| | | | | M S V | M S V |

## RUNNING RECORD

| Page # | Running Record | Count | | Information Used | |
|---|---|---|---|---|---|
| | | E | SC | E<br>M S V | SC<br>M S V |

<br><br>

**Comprehension Conversation** Discuss the text, asking questions that reveal the student's literal comprehension (recall) and deeper comprehension (inferential thinking). Notes/Observations:

<br><br>

### Fluency and Comprehension

| Rating | Fluency | Rating | Literal Comprehension | Rating | Deeper Comprehension |
|---|---|---|---|---|---|
| 0 | Slow or choppy word-by-word reading with no expression. | 0 | Recalls no important facts/events. | 0 | Shows no understanding of inferences or deeper meaning. |
| 1 | Moderately slow reading with 2 or 3 words grouped together. Little expression. | 1 | Recalls a limited number of important facts/events. | 1 | Shows limited understanding of inferences or deeper meaning. |
| 2 | Acceptable reading rate with 3 to 4 words grouped in meaningful phrases most of the time. Some expression. | 2 | Recalls some important facts/events. | 2 | Shows some understanding of inferences or deeper meaning. |
| 3 | Phrased and fluent reading with appropriate intonation and expression. | 3 | Recalls most of the important facts/events. | 3 | Shows full understanding of inferences or deeper meaning. |

| Trace It | Write It | Don't Look at It |
|---|---|---|
| | | |

# INDEX